BOUNDARIES

WORKBOOK

Resources by Henry Cloud and John Townsend

Books

Boundaries (and workbook)
Boundaries in Dating (and workbook)
Boundaries in Marriage (and workbook)
Boundaries with Kids (and workbook)
Boundaries with Teens (Townsend)
Changes That Heal (and workbook) (Cloud)
Hiding from Love (Townsend)
How People Grow (and workbook)
How to Have That Difficult Conversation You've Been Avoiding
Making Small Groups Work
The Mom Factor (and workbook)
Raising Great Kids
Raising Great Kids Workbook for Parents of Preschoolers
Raising Great Kids Workbook for Parents of School-Age Children
Raising Great Kids Workbook for Parents of Teenagers
Safe People (and workbook)
12 "Christian" Beliefs That Can Drive You Crazy

Video Curriculum

Boundaries
Boundaries in Dating
Boundaries in Marriage
Boundaries with Kids
Raising Great Kids for Parents of Preschoolers
ReGroup (with Bill Donahue)

Audio

Boundaries
Boundaries in Dating
Boundaries in Marriage
Boundaries with Kids
Boundaries with Teens (Townsend)
Changes That Heal (Cloud)
How People Grow
How to Have That Difficult Conversation You've Been Avoiding
Making Small Groups Work
The Mom Factor
Raising Great Kids

BOUNDARIES
WORKBOOK

WHEN TO SAY YES
HOW TO SAY NO
TO TAKE CONTROL
OF YOUR LIFE

DR. HENRY CLOUD & DR. JOHN TOWNSEND

ZONDERVAN®

ZONDERVAN.com/
AUTHORTRACKER
follow your favorite authors

Boundaries Workbook
Copyright © 1995 by Henry Cloud and John Townsend

Requests for information should be addressed to:

Zondervan, *Grand Rapids, Michigan 49530*

ISBN 978-0-310-49481-2

Published in association with Yates & Yates, www.yates2.com

Edited by Lisa Guest

Printed in the United States of America

10 11 12 13 • 78 77 76 75 74 73 72 71 70 69 68 67 66 65 64 63 62 61 60 59 58 57 56

Contents

Introduction

One of the most serious problems facing Christians today is confusion about boundaries. Many sincere, dedicated believers struggle with tremendous confusion about when it is biblically appropriate to set limits. When confronted with their lack of boundaries, they raise good questions:

Can I set limits and still be a loving person?
What are legitimate boundaries?
What if someone is upset or hurt by my boundaries?
How do I answer someone who wants my time, love, energy, or money?
Why do I feel guilty or afraid when I consider setting boundaries?
How do boundaries relate to submission?
Aren't boundaries selfish?
Why is it difficult for me to hear no from other people?
Why do I tend to want to control other people when I don't get what I want?

Just as homeowners set physical property lines around their land, we need to set mental, physical, emotional, and spiritual boundaries for our lives to help us distinguish what is our responsibility and what is not. The inability to set appropriate boundaries at appropriate times with the appropriate people can be very destructive.

Misinformation about what the Bible says about boundaries can also be destructive. To counter such wrong thinking, this study guide and the accompanying text present a biblical view of boundaries: what they are, what they protect, how they are developed, how they are injured, how to repair them, and how to use them. As you read the book and work through this guide, you will find answers to the questions listed above—and more. In fact, our goal is to help you use biblical boundaries appropriately to achieve the relationships and purposes that God intends for you as you grow in him.

Dr. Henry Cloud
Dr. John Townsend
Newport Beach,
California

Part One

What Are Boundaries?

Chapter 1

What Does a Boundary Look Like?

Give Me Something to Hope For

It's sometimes easier to see in other people the very thing we would do well to change in ourselves. Look again at Sherrie's day. Read through the entries from 6:00 a.m. to 11:50 p.m. and see how closely your life resembles her boundaryless day (pp. 15–26).*

- Where do you see yourself in Sherrie's actions and thoughts? Be as specific as possible.

- Who in your life could be cast in the role of Sherrie's mother (p. 16); her husband, Walt (pp. 17, 23–25); her "friend," Lois (p. 18); her demanding boss, Jeff (p. 19); the encouraging teacher, Mrs. Russell (pp. 20–21); her unreachable daughter (p. 21); and the church leader with yet another request (pp. 22–23)? Who treats you the way these people treated Sherrie? Whose words and actions elicit the same kind of response (emotional and otherwise) from you that these people elicited from Sherrie?

---

* All page numbers in this workbook refer to the page numbers of the original book, *Boundaries*. When no page references are given for italicized text, it usually means that these sections are additional thoughts of the author on that particular topic.

- How did you respond to the way Sherrie used Scripture as she made decisions that violated her—at best—shaky boundaries?

- If Sherrie came to you for advice, what would you say to her? How would you diagnose her problem? Which of your own words of advice would you do well to heed?

You can probably identify with Sherrie's dilemma—her isolation, her helplessness, her confusion, her guilt, and, above all, her sense that her life is out of control. Trying harder isn't working for her. Being nice out of fear isn't working for her. Taking responsibility for others isn't working for her. Sherrie still suffers severely from her inability to take ownership of her life. She has great difficulty knowing what things are *her responsibility and what things* are not. *In her desire to do the right thing or to avoid conflict, she ends up taking on problems that God never intended her to take on (pp. 26–28).*

- Look at your life through this lens. What problems have you taken on that God may never have intended you to take on?

- What motivated you to take on those problems you just listed—your desire to do the right thing, your efforts to avoid conflict, your fear of disappointing someone or not being liked, a sense of guilt, an inner "should," or something else?

Any confusion about responsibility and ownership in our lives is a problem of boundaries (p. 27).

- Why are you confused about boundaries—about when and how to draw them for yourself or even whether drawing boundaries is okay? What has happened to foster that confusion?

- Why are Christians especially susceptible to confusion about boundaries?

The questions listed in the introduction and below reflect some of the confusion we Christians may have about boundaries.

> *Can I set limits and still be a loving person?*
> *What are legitimate boundaries?*
> *What if someone is upset or hurt by my boundaries?*
> *How do I answer someone who wants my time, love, energy, or money?*
> *Why do I feel guilty or afraid when I consider setting boundaries?*
> *How do boundaries relate to submission?*
> *Aren't boundaries selfish?*
> *Is it difficult for me to hear no from other people?*
> *Do I tend to want to control other people when I don't get what I want?*

- Which of these questions have you wondered about? Which questions do you especially want answers for?

- What do you want to gain from this study besides answers to those questions? What hopes and goals do you have for yourself?

As you proceed through this study and work toward the goals you have set for yourself, remember that this book aims to help you see the deeply biblical nature of boundaries as they operate in the character of God, his universe, and his people.

Remember, too, that our goal is to help you use biblical boundaries appropriately so that you can experience the relationships and achieve the purposes that God intends for you as his child.

A Little Boundary Clarification

Remember the story of Bill (pp. 29–31)? His parents paid his bills, fretted over his circumstances, worried about his future, and exerted much energy to keep him going. Bill didn't study, plan, or work, yet he had a nice place to live, plenty of money, and all the rights of a family member who was doing his part. He was irresponsible and happy—and they were responsible and miserable.

And remember how we helped his parents see that? We compared Bill to a man who never watered his lawn. Whenever his neighbors turned on their sprinkler system, the water fell on Bill's lawn. Their grass was turning brown and dying, but Bill saw his green grass and thought his yard was doing fine. We suggested that they define the property lines a little better and fix the sprinkler system so that water would fall on their own lawn. Perhaps then, when Bill didn't water his lawn and found himself living in dirt, he would recognize that he had a problem and would do something about it (p. 30).

- Where are you watering someone else's yard while your own grass withers and dies?

- Where are you letting someone else water your yard?

- Is it cruel to stop watering someone else's yard? Would it be cruel for the person who is watering your yard to stop? Why or why not?

14

Invisible Property Lines and Responsibility

In the physical world, boundaries are easy to see. In the spiritual world, boundaries are just as real, but often harder to see (p. 31).

• What boundaries in the physical world do you deal with every day?

• What kind of boundaries do you think need to exist in the spiritual world?

• Why are spiritual boundaries as important as physical boundaries?

The goal of this lesson is to help you define your intangible boundaries and to recognize them as an ever-present reality that can increase your love and save your life. These boundaries define your soul and help you guard and maintain it (Prov. 4:23) (p.31).

Me and Not Me

Boundaries define us. They define what is me *and* what is not me. *A boundary shows where you end and someone else begins, leading to a sense of ownership. We have to deal with what is in our soul (Prov. 14:10), and boundaries help us define what that is. The Bible tells us clearly what our parameters are and how to protect them, but often our family or other past relationships have confused us about our parameters (p. 32).*

• Explain how knowing what you are to own and take responsibility for gives you freedom.

15

- Why does pain result when we are not shown the parameters of our soul or are taught wrong parameters?

To and For

We are responsible to *others and* for *ourselves.*

- What does Galatians 6:2 teach about responsibility to others?

- When has someone in your life followed Christ's example of sacrificial love and denied himself or herself in order to do for you what you could not do for yourself?

- When have you followed Christ's example of sacrificial love and denied yourself in order to do for others what they could not do for themselves?

Now look at Galatians 6:5. The Greek words for burden *and* load *give important insight into these two verses.* Burden *means "excess burdens," boulders that we need help carrying.* Load *means "cargo" or "the burden of daily toil." These loads are like knapsacks. A knapsack is possible to carry, and we are expected to carry our own. We are expected to deal with our own feelings, attitudes, and behaviors, as well as the responsibilities God has given us, even though it takes effort. In addition, we are not to carry the knapsacks of others (Luke 9:23) (pp. 32–33).*

- When have you acted as if your "boulders" are your daily load and have refused help? Where are you doing this today?

- When have you acted as if your "daily load" is a boulder that you shouldn't have to carry? Where are you doing this today?

- What have these two questions helped you see about yourself—and what will you do with what you have learned?

In order to not stay in pain or become irresponsible, it is important that you determine what "me" is, where your boundary of responsibility lies, and where someone else's begins. Let's look more closely now at the nature of boundaries (p. 33).

Good In, Bad Out

Boundaries help us distinguish our property so that we can take care of it. We need to keep things that will nurture us inside our fences and keep things that will harm us outside. We need to keep the good in and the bad out, and that's what boundaries help us do (p. 33).

- The fences around our property—our boundaries—need gates in them so that we can let out the bad when it is inside. What pain and sin do you need to get out through confession so that it does not continue to poison you on the inside (Mark 7:21–23; James 5:16; 1 John 1:9)?

- We also need those gates to let in the good that may be on the outside. We need, for instance, to receive Jesus and his truth (John 1:12; Rev. 3:20). We also need to open up to the good things other people want to give us (2 Cor. 6:11–13). What good things—from Jesus and his people—would you like to be able to receive?

Clearly, boundaries are not meant to be walls. The Bible does not say that we are to be "walled off" from others; in fact, it says we are to be "one" with them (John 17:11). We are to be in community with one another, but in every community the members have their own space and property (p. 34).

- As a result of past injury, have you reversed the function of boundaries? Where are you using them to keep the bad in and the good out? What pain are you holding inside rather than expressing it and getting it out of your soul? Where are you not opening up to the love and support from the outside that would bring healing?

God and Boundaries

This concept of boundaries comes from the very nature of God. God defines himself as a distinct, separate being, and he is responsible for himself (p. 35).

- God defines his personality by telling us about himself. What does he tell us in the Bible about what he thinks, feels, plans, allows, doesn't allow, likes, and dislikes? See, for instance, Genesis 12:2; Jeremiah 3:12; Ezekiel 6:9; 36:26.

- God differentiates himself from his creation, from us, and from others. He tells us who he is and who he is not. What does he say about himself in Leviticus 11:44; Isaiah 48:12; 60:16; 1 John 4:16?

- God also limits what he will allow in his yard. What, for example, do Exodus 20:1 –17 and Matthew 5:21 – 6:4 say about those limits?

- What do Hosea 6:6, Micah 6:8, Mark 12:30–31, and 1 John 4:7–12 say about the gates in God's fences?

God also has boundaries within the Trinity. The Father, the Son, and the Spirit are one, but at the same time they are distinct persons with their own boundaries. Each has his own personhood and responsibilities, as well as a connection and love for one another (John 17:24). We, whom he created in his likeness and whom he gave personal responsibility within limits, need to develop boundaries like God's if we are to be effective stewards over the life he has given us (p. 35).

Examples of Boundaries

A boundary is anything that helps to differentiate you from someone else or shows where you begin and end (p. 35).

- Review the discussion of each type of boundary listed below (pp. 35–40). Then, for each one, note some biblical support (what does the Bible say or what example does it give for maintaining these boundaries?). Refer to a time when people honored that particular boundary of yours (what were the circumstances, why were you able to be strong, and what did you learn from this experience?), and consider what hinders you from keeping each boundary strong (look back at a time when people didn't honor your boundary and try to identify why).

  - Skin

  - Words, especially the word *no*

  - Truth

- Geographical distance

- Time

- Emotional distance

- Other people

- Consequences

- Now consider the list of boundaries from another perspective.
  - Which boundaries, when they are set by other people, do you need to do a better job honoring?

  - Why might you have a hard time honoring people's boundaries, especially certain ones?

- What will you do to be more respectful of the boundaries of the people in your life?

What's Within My Boundaries?

The story of the Good Samaritan (Luke 10:30–37) is a good illustration of when boundaries should be both observed and violated. The imaginary next chapter of the story, however, shows what happens when, moved with compassion to give to someone in need, we find ourselves manipulated into giving more than we want to give and, as a result, become resentful and angry—and sometimes we may be the ones doing the manipulating! That scenario can be avoided when we clearly understand what falls within our boundaries and what we are responsible for (pp. 40–42).

Feelings

Feelings should neither be ignored nor placed in charge. They are signals that alert us to be aware of the condition of our heart. The Bible says to "own" your feelings and be responsible for them. You must see them as your property so you can begin to find an answer to whatever issue they are pointing to. They can often motivate you to do much good (Matt. 9:36; 15:32; Luke 10:33; 15:20) (p. 42).

- What do you tend to do with your feelings—ignore them or let them be in charge? Why do you think you respond that way?

- What do you tend to do with feelings of anger?

- If you are nursing any feelings of anger right now, what problem that needs to be addressed are they pointing you toward? What will you do about that problem?

Attitudes and Beliefs

Attitudes have to do with your orientation toward something, the stance you take toward God, others, life, work, and relationships. Beliefs are anything you accept as true. Although you may struggle to set limits and accept appropriate responsibility, know that doing so will save lives (Prov. 13:18, 24) (pp. 42–43).

- You are the only one who feels the effects of your attitudes and beliefs, and you are the only one who can change those attitudes and beliefs. Which attitudes and beliefs that you hold are causing you to make poor choices or experience pain? What will you do to get those attitudes and beliefs in line with God's truth?

- Do you tend to feel responsible for other people's feelings, choices, and behaviors? In what areas of your life or for which people in your life do you do this? What will you do to gain a better understanding of what you really are responsible for?

Behaviors

Behaviors have consequences. As Paul says, "A man reaps what he sows" (Gal. 6:7–8). As Proverbs warns, "stern discipline awaits him who leaves the path" (15:10). To rescue people from the natural consequences of their behavior is to render them powerless (p. 43).

- When has someone interrupted the law of sowing and reaping in your life and protected you from consequences that could have been good teachers? What happened?

- When have you interrupted the law of sowing and reaping in someone's life and protected that person from consequences that could have been good teachers? What happened?

Choices

We need to take responsibility for our choices. Doing so leads to the fruit of self-control (Gal. 5:23). A common boundary problem is disowning our choices and trying to lay the responsibility for them on someone else. Throughout the Scriptures, people are reminded of their choices and asked to take responsibility for them (Josh. 24:15; Matt. 20:13; Rom. 8:13; 2 Cor. 9:7; Philem. 14) (pp. 44–45).

- How often do you use the phrases "I had to" or "He/she made me" when you explain why you did or didn't do something?

- What choices in your life have you failed to take responsibility for? Whom are you blaming for what circumstances of your life?

Values

What we value is what we love and assign importance to. Often we do not take responsibility for what we value. Boundaries help us not to deny but to own our old hurtful boundaries so that God can create a new heart in us, a heart that values things that will satisfy and things that will last (p. 45).

- When have you been caught up in valuing the approval of people rather than the approval of God (John 12:43)? What lesson did you learn from that experience or from seeing someone else caught in that trap?

- Where might you be seeking power, riches, or pleasure in an attempt to satisfy your deepest longing, which is really for love? How would taking responsibility for loving the wrong things affect your life?

Limits

Two aspects of limits are important for creating better boundaries. First, setting limits and separating ourselves protects love because we are taking a stand against things that destroy love. Second, setting limits in order to establish an internal structure is an important component of boundaries and identity, as well as ownership, responsibility, and self-control (pp. 45–46).

- The first aspect is setting limits with others. That means setting limits on our exposure to people who are behaving poorly, and God is our model for doing so (Matt. 18:15–17; 1 Cor. 5:9–13). We can't change other people or make them behave right, but we can gain some distance from them. Where in your life today would you do well to limit your exposure to someone? Why would that be a wise move? What is keeping you from doing so?

- Like setting limits with others, setting our own internal limits helps us create better boundaries. We need self-control without repression. What destructive desires do you need to learn to say no to? What good desires do you need to learn to say no to because the timing isn't right?

Talents

Although it uses money as an example, Matthew 25:14–30 clearly illustrates our God-ordained responsibility for ownership and use of our talents and gifts. Our talents are within our boundaries and are our responsibility, yet taking ownership of them is often frightening and always risky. It takes work, practice, learning, prayer, resources, and grace to overcome the fear of failure that can keep us from exercising our talents, but we are accountable—and much happier—when we exercise our God-given gifts and are productive (pp. 46–47).

- What talents, gifts, and abilities has God given you? If you're not sure, ask someone who knows you well to help you identify them.

- What talents, gifts, and abilities are you currently exercising? How do you feel about what you are doing?

- What talents, gifts, or abilities are you afraid to exercise? What is the root of those fears? What steps will you take to overcome those fears?

Thoughts

Our minds and thoughts are important reflections of the image of God. We are called to love God with all our mind (Mark 12:30), and we are to "take captive every thought to make it obedient to Christ" (2 Cor. 10:5). We must have our own thoughts, we must keep learning about God, we must clarify any distorted ideas, and if we want others to know what we're thinking, we must tell them (pp. 47–48).

- We must own our own thoughts. Do you think things through for yourself, or do you tend to accept other people's ideas and let them do your thinking for you? Why? Name one area of your life where you would do well to think through some issues for yourself.

- We must grow in knowledge and expand our minds. What are you doing to grow in your knowledge of God and his Word? Of God and his creation? How are you using your brain to glorify God?

- We must clarify distorted thinking, and the easiest distortions to notice are those in personal relationships. Consider past relationships. Where do you see now that you had distorted ideas about the person involved? Where might you now be failing to see people as they really are?

- Finally, we need to make sure that we are communicating our thoughts to others. After all, "who among men knows the thoughts of a man except the man's spirit within him?" (1 Cor. 2:11). Whom are you expecting to be able to read your mind? To whom are you afraid to communicate your thoughts? What do you think keeps you from doing so?

Desires

Each of us has different desires and wants, dreams and wishes, goals and plans, hungers and thirsts—but few of us are satisfied. One reason is that we lack the internal structure that boundaries provide to enable us to define and then take the specific steps necessary to reach our goals. Furthermore, we often do not actively seek our desires from God (Ecc. 11:9; Matt. 7:7–11; Phil. 2:12–13; James 4:2–3). Yet God is truly interested in our desires. He made them, and "he fulfills the desires of those who fear him" (Ps. 145:19; see also Ps. 21:2–3; 37:4) (pp. 48–49).

- When have you experienced the fulfillment of a God-given desire? Be specific about the circumstances and your feelings.

- What desires are you currently pursuing that your heavenly Father, wise parent that he is, is probably not interested in giving you?

- Consider the desires, dreams, and goals that you are currently pursuing. Make them the focus of some prayer time, asking God to refine your ideas and redirect you where necessary.

Love

Our ability to give and respond to love is our greatest gift. The heart that God has fashioned in his image is the center of our being. Its abilities to open up to love and to allow love to flow outward are crucial to life. We need to claim our hearts as our property and work on our weaknesses, whether we are weak receiving, or weak giving, love. Doing so will open up life to us (pp. 49–50).

- Why might you have difficulty giving and/or receiving love?

- Our loving heart, like our physical one, needs an inflow as well as an outflow of lifeblood (Matt. 22:37, 39; 2 Cor. 6:11–13). How healthy is the inflow in your life? What healthy, godly relationships nurture you?

- How healthy is the outflow of love in your life? Where are you giving to others the kind of unconditional love God has given you?

- What do your answers to the previous two questions tell you about the condition of your trust muscle? Are you resisting love and/or failing to give love because it's hard for you to trust?

Feelings, attitudes and beliefs, behaviors, choices, values, limits, talents, thoughts, desires, and love—all of these lie within our boundaries. We therefore need to take responsibility for all of these areas of our souls.

- In which of these areas are you doing a fairly good job taking responsibility?

- In what area will you start working to take more responsibility this week? What will you do? Be specific.

Taking care of all that lies within our boundaries isn't easy. Neither is allowing other people to take care of what lies within their boundaries. Setting boundaries and maintaining them is hard work. But, as you'll see in the next lesson, boundary problems take on recognizable shapes. Recognizing the shape of your boundary problems can help you establish healthy boundaries for yourself.

Prayer

Father God, you have seen where my life resembles Sherrie's — where I have failed to establish boundaries, where I have failed to build "gates" in my "fences," and where I am keeping out good and keeping in bad. You also know the reasons for these things — the past hurts, the poor models, the misunderstood Christian teachings. And you know, too, the hope I've found in these pages as I've realized that you call me to establish boundaries and that you yourself model them for me. Teach me, as I proceed through this study, to take responsibility for my feelings, attitudes and beliefs, behaviors, choices, values, limits, talents, thoughts, desires, and love. Help me establish appropriate and biblical boundaries so that I may glorify you with my life. I pray in Jesus' name. Amen.

Chapter 2

Understanding Boundaries

It's easy to misunderstand boundaries. We readily see, for instance, that people who have difficulty setting limits have a boundary problem, but so do those who don't respect other people's limits. In this lesson we'll categorize the main types of boundary problems to help you identify weaknesses in your own boundaries (p. 51).

Compliants: Saying "Yes" to the Bad

Compliant people have fuzzy and indistinct boundaries; they "melt" into the demands and needs of other people. Compliants are chameleons. Their inability to say no to the bad is pervasive, and it keeps them from refusing and even recognizing evil. Their spiritual and emotional "radar" is broken; they have no ability to guard their hearts (Prov. 4:23) (pp. 51–53).

• As you were growing up, what did you learn about setting boundaries and saying no? Were those things good or bad? How did you learn that?

• When have you noticed that your spiritual and emotional "radar" isn't functioning well? When, for instance, have you recognized evil only in retrospect?

- Adults whose radar is broken say yes to bad things. What bad things have you said yes to? What bad things are you saying yes to now?

- If you are a compliant, there are several reasons why the word *no* seems to get stuck in your throat whenever you need to protect yourself. Which of the following reasons are true for you?
  - Fear of hurting the other person's feelings
  - Fear of abandonment and separateness
  - A wish to be totally dependent on another person
  - Fear of someone else's anger
  - Fear of punishment
  - Fear of being shamed
  - Fear of being seen as bad or selfish
  - Fear of being unspiritual
  - Fear of your own overstrict, critical conscience

Fear of your own conscience is actually experienced as guilt (1 Cor. 8:7). That overstrict conscience is your unbiblical and critical internal parent whom you are afraid to confront and who is behind your self-condemnation (p. 53).

- Do you condemn yourself for things that God does not condemn you for? Give an example.

- When have you obeyed your harsh conscience in order to avoid the additional guilt that would come with confronting someone? Be specific.

Biblical obedience needs to be distinguished from compliance motivated by a harsh internalized parent voice. Compliants take on too many responsibilities and set too few boundaries, not by choice, but because they are afraid (p. 54).

- When has compassion motivated you to say yes or no to some responsibility? How did you feel about taking on that additional responsibility? Can you see the difference between being motivated by compassion and being motivated by guilt?

- When have you been compliant on the outside and resentful on the inside as you said yes to some responsibility?

- Evaluate your life today. Have you assumed most of your responsibilities out of "compassion, and not sacrifice" (Matt. 9:13 NASB)? Or have guilt and your internalized parent voice been behind many of your current responsibilities? Be honest with yourself.

- What might you do next time someone asks you to take on additional responsibilities?

Avoidants: Saying "No" to the Good

Avoidance is the inability to ask for help, to recognize one's own needs, and to let others in. Avoidants withdraw when they are in need; they do not ask for the support of other people. Those who are like Rachel avoid opportunities for others to love them as they have loved others (pp. 54–55).

Boundaries are supposed to be fences with gates that let the good in and the bad out; boundaries are not supposed to be walls (p. 55).

- Are your boundaries more like walls than fences? Explain why you answered as you did.

- God designed our personal boundaries to have gates. He even allows us the freedom to let him in or close him off (Rev. 3:20). When it comes to God, do your boundaries function like walls or like fences with gates? Support your answer with specific details from your life.

- The impermeable boundaries of avoidants cause a rigid unacceptance of their God-given needs. Do you experience your problems and legitimate needs and wants as something bad, destructive, or shameful? Where do you think you learned that?

Remember Marti? She said yes when someone needed four hours with her and, by failing to ask for help when she needed it, said no to the support from other people. Marti said yes to the bad (compliant) and no to the good (avoidant). Avoidants and especially compliant avoidants can feel drained. They are unable to receive the support they need to replace the energy they expend in their day-to-day life (p. 55).

- Do you, like Marti, have reversed boundaries? Do you have boundaries where you shouldn't have them but no boundaries where you need them?

- Be specific now. Where do you have boundaries where you don't need them? Where do you need boundaries but don't yet have them?

Controllers: Not Respecting Others' Boundaries

Controllers see a person's no as a challenge to change his or her mind. Controllers can't respect other people's limits. They resist taking responsibility for their own lives, so they need to control other people's lives. Controllers are therefore perceived as manipulative and aggressive bullies (pp. 56–59).

- In what relationships or situations have you been perceived as a controller? Why was it important for you to have control in that situation?

The primary problem of individuals who can't hear no is that they tend to project responsibility for their lives onto others. They use various means of control to motivate others to carry the load God intends to be theirs alone. These controllers come in two types (p. 57).

Aggressive controllers clearly don't listen to, or respect, other people's boundaries. They are sometimes verbally abusive and sometimes physically abusive, but most of the time they simply aren't aware that others even have boundaries. In the Bible, Peter is an example of an aggressive controller. Peter didn't want to accept the Lord's boundaries, and Jesus immediately confronted Peter's violation of his boundaries (Mark 8:33) (p. 57).

- When have you come up against an aggressive controller? What did he or she demand of you? How did you respond and how did you feel?

- An aggressive controller attempts to get others to change. They neglect their own responsibility to accept others as they are. When have you been guilty of this?

- When have you felt an aggressive controller's failure to accept you as you are? How did you deal with this?

Manipulative controllers are less honest than aggressive controllers. Manipulators try to persuade people out of their boundaries; they talk others into yes. They use guilt messages, manipulate circumstances, and seduce others into carrying their burdens (pp. 57–58).

- When have you come up against a manipulative controller? What did he or she do to turn your no into a yes?

- Manipulators deny their desires to control others, brush aside their own self-centeredness, and admit no wrong (Prov. 30:20). Which of these elements did you see in the situation you just referred to?

- When, if ever, have you been a manipulative controller? Why did you take that approach at that time?

Compliants and avoidants can also be controllers. One way they do this is by doing a favor for a friend in the hopes that they'll receive love in return (p. 58).

- When have you acted lovingly in hopes that you'd be loved in return? Did you receive the love you wanted?

- When have you received a favor only to find that you've hurt that person's feelings by not figuring out the price tag attached?

learly, controllers do a lot of damage to other people, but they themselves have boundary problems as well. Undisciplined, they have little ability to delay gratification, and that's why another person's no is hard for them to hear. Controllers are also limited in their ability to take responsibility for owning their lives: they bully or manipulate to get others' help because they can't function on their own. Finally, controllers are isolated. They rarely feel loved because the people around them are there out of fear, guilt, or dependency. Controllers can't terrorize or make others feel guilty and be loved by them at the same time (pp. 58–59). At some deep level, controllers are aware of their isolation.

- If you've seen yourself in this description of a controller, which boundary problems listed above do you exhibit as a controller?

- This description of boundary problems may make you feel more compassion toward the controllers in your life. What might you do, however, to protect your boundaries from those people who have no respect for them?

Nonresponsives: Not Hearing the Needs of Others

Termed "nonresponsives," these individuals do not pay attention to the responsibilities of love. We are responsible to care about and help, within certain limits, people whom God places in our lives (Prov. 3:27; Rom. 12:18). While we shouldn't take on the responsibility of others' feelings, attitudes, and behaviors, we do have certain responsibilities to each other. That's why the issue with nonresponsives is more than just insensitivity (pp. 59–61).

- When have you been a nonresponsive and failed to act according to your responsibilities to another person?

Nonresponsives fall into one of two groups. Those with a critical spirit toward others' needs hate being incomplete in themselves and therefore ignore the needs of others. Other nonresponsives, guilty of a form of narcissism, are so absorbed in their own desires and needs that they exclude others (p. 60).

- If you tend to be a nonresponsive, which group do you fall into? Why do you think you're in that group?

- When have you come up against a nonresponsive? What kind of response had you hoped for, and what kind of response did you receive?

- Do you think that the nonresponsive was critical or self-absorbed? What makes you think so?

It's important that you don't confuse a nonresponsive's narcissistic self-absorption with a person's God-given sense of responsibility for taking care of his or her own needs first so that he or she is able to love others (Phil. 2:4) (pp. 60–61).

- God wants us to take care of ourselves so that we can help others without moving into a crisis ourselves. How good are you at taking care of yourself?

- How does taking care of yourself or not taking care of yourself affect your ability and willingness to help other people?

Turn to page 61 of the text and look at the "Summary of Boundary Problems." This chart may help you see the kinds of problems with which you struggle. The rest of the book will help you deal with these problems.

- In which quadrant do you see yourself?

- In which quadrants would you categorize the people you are struggling with today?

Functional and Relational Boundary Issues

A final boundary problem involves the distinction between functional and relational boundaries. "Functional boundaries" refers to a person's ability to complete a task, project, or job. It has to do with performance, discipline, initiative, and planning. "Relational boundaries" refers to the ability to speak truth to others with whom we are in relationship (p. 62).

- How clearly defined and solid are your functional boundaries?
  - How competent are you when it comes to completing a task?

  - Do you, like Jesus' friend Martha, tend to do the wrong thing at the wrong time (Luke 10:42)?

  - To what do you credit your success or your struggle with functional boundaries?

- How well established are your relational boundaries?
  - Do you have a relatively easy time being honest with your friends? How easy would it be for you to tell a friend that you don't like his or her chronic lateness?

  - To what do you credit your success or your struggle with relational boundaries?

- Do you have good functional boundaries, but poor relational boundaries? Or do you have good relational boundaries, but poor functional boundaries? Why do you think your strengths and weaknesses in boundaries are where they are?

In the first half of this lesson, we've taken a look at the main types of boundary problems, and you may now have a clearer idea why you struggle as you do. Share what you've learned with the Lord.

Father God, I've realized that I'm a/an . . .

- **Compliant.** I need you, Lord, to teach me to say no. I need you to repair my spiritual and emotional "radar." And I need you to help me overcome the reasons why the word "no" gets stuck in my throat and to mature my overstrict conscience. I also ask you to guide me the next time someone asks me to take on another responsibility. If I say yes, may it be because I'm answering your call and not because I'm acting out of fear.

- **Avoidant.** I need you, Lord, to help me let other people—and you—into my life. Show me where my boundaries are more like walls than fences, where I need to build gates, and where I need to establish boundaries where there aren't any. Replace my wrong perspective on my needs with your truth, the truth that we human beings have needs, that we need one another and that we need you.

- **Controller.** I need you, Lord, to forgive me for not respecting other people's boundaries and for not accepting them as they are. Forgive me where I've been aggressive, abusive, and manipulative, and give me the courage to apologize to those I have hurt. And, God, heal me. You know the hurt and the fear out of which these controlling behaviors grow. You also know the isolation I feel. Please help me, God.

- **Nonresponsive.** I need you, Lord, to forgive me for my insensitivity, my critical nature, and my self-absorption. Teach me, God, the responsibilities of love so that I may extend to the people in my life the love you have so graciously extended to me.

Father God, you know the "doing" (functional) and "being" (relational) boundary problems I am dealing with as well. Teach me to have the discipline, initiative, and planning skills I need to complete projects and tasks, and give me the ability to speak the truth in love to those with whom I am in relationship.

I have so much to learn, God, and I am thankful for the opportunity to do so. Please be with me along the way. I pray in Jesus' name. Amen.

Boundary Development

Having looked at boundary problems, let's now consider how to develop strong and healthy boundaries. Why do some people seem to have natural boundaries and others have no boundaries at all? The chapter "How Boundaries Are Developed" reveals that our boundaries have a lot to do with the family in which we grew up (pp. 63–64).

- Remember Jim, the man who was "Mr. Can Do" at the office and "The Phantom" at home? Review his story (pp. 63–64). At what points are you and Jim a lot alike?

Jim's problems didn't start the day he was married. They developed during his early significant relationships and became a part of his character structure then. As you work through the rest of this lesson, you'll begin to understand where your own boundaries started crumbling or became set in concrete—and how to repair them (pp. 63–64).

Boundaries aren't inherited; they are built. To be the truth-telling, responsible, free, and loving people God wants us to be, we need to learn limits in childhood, when our character is being formed. Good parents help children reach that goal (pp. 64–65).

- What instruction does Proverbs 22:6 give parents?

- What does this verse mean—and what is it commonly misunderstood to mean?

The Bible teaches that we pass through life in stages and that each stage has distinct tasks to perform (p. 65).

- What does 1 John 2:12–13 suggest about these stages of development?

Bonding: The Foundation of Boundary Building

Our deepest need is to belong, to be in a relationship, to have a spiritual and emotional "home." It is the very nature of God to be in relationship. The apostle John writes, "God is love" (1 John 4:16), and love means relationship—the caring, committed connection of one individual to another (p. 66).

- When did you realize what Wendy's struggle (pp. 65–66) illustrates that you can't develop or set boundaries apart from supportive relationships with God and, just as important, with other people? What circumstances helped or are helping you learn this truth?

- In Genesis 2:18, what observation about human beings does God make?

We are built for relationship. Attachment is the foundation of the soul's existence. When this foundation is cracked or faulty, boundaries become impossible to develop. Why? Because when we lack relationship, we have nowhere to go in a conflict. We live in a vacuum. When we are not secure that we are loved, we are forced to choose between two bad options—setting limits at the risk of losing a relationship, or not setting limits and remaining a prisoner to the wishes of another person (p. 66).

- Which scenes from your own life, past or present, does the first option remind you of?

- Which scenes from your own life, past or present, does the second option remind you of?

When infants successfully complete the first developmental task—that of bonding with Mom and Dad—they gain the security that comes with knowing they are loved. They develop an internal sense of belonging and safety even away from the presence of their mother. As children learn to feel safe and at home with their primary relationships, they are building good foundations to withstand the separateness and conflict that come with boundary development. It is God's plan for us to be loved enough by him and others so that we don't feel isolated even when we are alone (p. 67).

- What phrases from Ephesians 3:17 and Colossians 2:7 refer to this kind of emotional object constancy?

- How does this inner sense of security regarding a parent's love facilitate the development of a relationship with God?

- Knowing what you do about your infancy and your struggles with boundaries today, comment on how well you completed the task of bonding. What factors may have interfered with bonding?

Separation and Individuation: The Construction of a Soul

As infants gain a sense of internal safety and attachment, a second need arises. The baby's need for separation (perceiving himself or herself as distinct from Mother, a "not-me" experience) and individuation (developing an identity, a "me" experience) starts to emerge (p. 68).

- Look again at young Jesus in Luke 2:41–49.

  - What evidence do you see here of separation?

  - And of individuation?

In this scene, the only one recorded from Jesus' boyhood, we see a young man who knows who he is and who he is not. He has separated from his folks and individuated in his values, thoughts, and opinions. Three phases are critical to this kind of separation and individuation and to the development of healthy boundaries in childhood: hatching, practicing, and rapprochement (pp. 69–76).

- Briefly summarize what goes on in each of the three phases of separation and individuation:

  - Hatching:

  - Practicing:

  - Rapprochement:

- Having read about the three phases of separation and individuation, comment on how well you—and your parents—did during:

  - The first three years of your life:

  - Your childhood:

  - Your adolescence:

Boundary Injuries: What Goes Wrong?

Boundary problems are rooted in thousands of encounters with others as well as in our own nature and personality (p. 76).

- What attitude toward boundaries was modeled in the home in which you grew up?

Consider now some of the ways your boundaries may have been injured.

Withdrawal from Boundaries

Good relationships and mature characters are built on appropriate nos. Developing children need to know their boundaries will be honored. It is crucial that their disagreements, their practices, and their experimentation not result in a withdrawal of love (p. 76).

- Who, if anyone, has withdrawn in response to your boundaries?

- When, if ever, have you withdrawn in response to other people's boundaries?

- What does Proverbs 27:17 say about the importance of not withdrawing when someone sets a boundary that we don't like?

Hostility Against Boundaries

When parents greet their children's disagreement, disobedience, or practicing with hostility, the children don't learn that delaying gratification and being responsible have benefits. They only learn how to avoid someone's wrath (pp. 78–80).

- Who, if anyone, has responded to your boundaries with hostility?

- When, if ever, have you responded with hostility to other people's boundaries?

- Hostility is a poor substitute for God's program for learning discipline. What does Hebrews 12:10–11 say about the importance and long-term effects of discipline?

Overcontrol

Overcontrol occurs when otherwise loving parents try to protect their children from making mistakes by having too-strict rules and limits (p. 80).

- On what issues did your parents exercise overcontrol?

- If you are a parent, on what issues may you be exercising too much control?

- Parents must make room for their children to make mistakes. What does Hebrews 5:14 say about the learning and development that occur because of the mistakes we make?

Lack of Limits

Lack of parental boundaries is the opposite of hostility, but the injuries that result can be just as severe (pp. 80–82).

- What areas of your life had too few limits?

- If you are a parent, are you failing to put limits on your children? Where?

- According to the warning of Matthew 25:14–30, what awaits a person living in an undisciplined, careless manner?

Inconsistent Limits

Sometimes, due to their confusion about rearing children or their own injuries, some parents combine strict and lax limits, sending conflicting messages to children (p. 82).

- Who, if anyone, offered you inconsistent limits? What conflicting messages did you hear?

- If you are a parent, what, if any, strict limits are you combining with lax ones?

- What phrase in James 1:6 might be used to describe the experience of a child raised with inconsistent limits?

Trauma

Specific traumas—emotional, physical, and sexual abuse, accidents and debilitating illnesses, death, divorce, or any other intensely painful experience—can injure boundary development (pp. 82–83).

- What, if any, trauma may have affected your boundaries?

- If you are a parent, what, if any, trauma may your child have experienced, despite your best efforts?

- In Isaiah 61:1, what words of hope does God speak to people who have experienced trauma?

Our Own Character Traits

We contribute to our boundary issues by our own individual character styles (p. 84).

- What character traits affect your boundaries? Do you, for instance, tend to be active and confrontational or quiet and reflective? Are you timid or weak (1 Thess. 5:14)?

- If you are a parent, what character traits do you see in your children that suggest how they will deal with life and address boundary issues?

Our Own Sinfulness

We also contribute to our boundary development problems by our own depravity (p. 84).

- What do Romans 3:23 and 8:2 teach about our sinfulness?

- How has your sinful nature—for instance, your resistance to submit to God, your resistance to humility—contributed to your boundary problems?

Now that you are gaining a clearer picture of what goes into boundary problems and boundary development, it's time to look at what the Bible says about how boundaries should operate and how they can be developed all through our lives. We'll do that in the next lesson.

Prayer

Heavenly Father, as I pause to consider the condition of my boundaries, I ask you to shed light on my past. Help me to see clearly the significant relationships and the forces that have contributed to my boundary struggles. Teach me from the past. Help me to find safe relationships where I can connect to the anger, the hurt, and the grief I may not have felt along the way. In your time, enable me also to extend for-giveness where it's needed. (For parents) Lord, I look to you for wisdom and guidance as I raise my children. Protect them, God, and heal the hurts they have already sustained. Show me—for the sake of the children you have entrusted to me as well for my own growth—the path to healthy boundaries. I pray in Jesus' name. Amen.

Chapter 3

Ten Laws of Boundaries

Like the alien described at the beginning of the chapter, people raised in dysfunctional families, or families where God's ways of boundaries are not practiced, find themselves lost, confused, and easily hurt in adult life. They don't understand the spiritual principles that govern relationships and personal well-being. Those principles—the spiritual realities that God built into the world he created—have never been explained to them, so they become prisoners of their own ignorance. We need to know these principles and operate according to them. In this lesson we'll look at ten laws of boundaries that, once learned, can help you begin to experience life differently (pp. 85–86).

Law #1: The Law of Sowing and Reaping

The law of cause and effect is a basic law of life. The Bible calls it the Law of Sowing and Reaping. When God tells us that we will reap what we sow, he is not punishing us; he's telling us how things really are (p. 86).

- In Galatians 6:7–8, what does Paul teach about sowing and reaping?

- What, if anything, have you sown "to [your] own flesh" (overeating, acting out, overspending, selfishness, ignoring of God's commandments, etc.), and what did you reap as a result?

- What positive seeds (eating right, exercising regularly, budgeting wisely, etc.) have you sown in your life and what are you reaping as a result?

Sometimes, however, we don't reap what we sow because someone steps in and reaps the consequences for us. The Law of Sowing and Reaping can be interrupted, and it is often people who have no boundaries who do the interrupting. Boundaries force the person who is doing the sowing to also do the reaping (p. 87).

- When has someone stepped in and rescued you from the consequences of your actions?

- When have you been the rescuer? Why did you step in?

Today we call a person who continually rescues another person a codependent. Often such a person will confront the irresponsible person (p. 87).

- When have you tried to confront the person you've rescued about his or her irresponsible behavior? What resulted from the confrontation?

- When has a rescuer confronted you about your behavior? What changes did you make as a result of that discussion?

As your answers to the preceding two questions probably reveal, confronting an irresponsible person is not painful to him; only consequences are. In fact, the Bible tells us it is worthless to confront foolish people (Prov. 9:8), and people caught in destructive patterns are usually more foolish than wise (p. 88).

- When have you seen consequences prompt someone to make important changes in his or her life?

- When have consequences for your actions prompted you to make changes in your own life?

Codependent people bring insults and pain onto themselves when they confront irresponsible people. In reality, they just need to stop interrupting the law of sowing and reaping (p. 88).

- Where do you need to stop interrupting the law of sowing and reaping in someone's life?

Law #2: The Law of Responsibility

People react in various ways to a talk on boundaries and taking responsibility for their own lives. Some respond with, "That's so self-centered. We should love one another and deny ourselves." Other people set out on a selfish and self-centered life, and still others begin to feel "guilty" when they do someone a favor (pp. 88–89).

- Which of these unbiblical views of responsibility reflect your initial response to the idea of boundaries?

The Law of Responsibility includes loving others. In fact, the commandment to love is the entire law for Christians (Gal. 5:13–14). Any time you are not loving others, you are not taking full responsibility for yourself: you have disowned your heart (p. 88).

- What does Jesus teach in John 15:12?

Problems arise when boundaries of responsibility are confused. We are to love one another, not be one another. We can't, for instance, grow for one another (p. 88).

- What biblical mandate for personal growth do you find in Philippians 2:12–13?

- What are you doing to take responsibility for your personal and spiritual growth?

- Where are you trying to take responsibility for someone else's personal and spiritual growth?

The Bible teaches that we are to treat others the way we would want to be treated (Matt. 7:12) (p. 89).

- How do our boundaries enable us to respond to this teaching?

- In light of Matthew 7:12, how are we to respond to people whose boundaries aren't well defined?

Another aspect of being responsible to *someone is setting limits on that person's destructive and irresponsible behavior. When you rescue someone from the consequences of their sin, you'll only have to do so again (Prov. 19:19). Throughout its pages, the Bible stresses that you are to give to needs and put limits on sin (Prov. 23:13–14). Boundaries help you do just that (p. 89).*

- Where have you seen this truth evident in real life?

- When have you been hurt or hurt someone else because limits were not put on behavior?

Law #3: The Law of Power

- Which, if any, of the following questions have you asked yourself:
  - Am I powerless over my behavior?
  - If I am, how can I become responsible?
  - What do I have the power to do?

Understanding the Law of Power will help you answer these questions. We are powerless over our addictions (pp. 89–91).

- Read through what Paul says in Romans 7:15–23. What phrases can you especially identify with?

- What specific struggles do the phrases you listed bring to mind?

Both the Bible and the Twelve Step program teach that people must admit that they are moral failures. The law of sin is at work within us, and we lie when we deny that fact (1 John 1:8) (p. 89).

Though you do not have the power in and of yourself to overcome your sinful patterns, you do have the power to do some things that will bring fruits of victory later (pp. 89–90).

1. *You have the power to agree with the truth about your problems (confession).*
2. *You have the power to submit your inability to God and turn your life over to him, the Doctor who can do what you are unable to do—bring about change (Matt. 5:3, 6; James 4:7–10; 1 John 1:9).*
3. *You have the power to ask God and others to reveal more and more about what is within your boundaries.*
4. *You have the power to turn from the evil that you find within you (repentance).*
5. *You have the power to humble yourself and ask God and others to help you with your developmental injuries and leftover childhood needs.*
6. *You have the power to seek out those whom you have injured and make amends.*
7. *You have the power to forgive those who have hurt you.*

• Which power(s) listed surprise you? Encourage you? Intimidate you?

• Which powers do you need to begin exercising in your life?

• What is the first step you will take to exercise one of the powers you just listed? Whom will you ask to help you?

Besides clarifying what you do have power over, boundaries help define what you do not have power over—everything outside of them! You can work on submitting yourself to the process of clarifying your boundaries and on working with

God to change you. You cannot change anything else: not the weather, the past, the economy, and especially not other people (pp. 90–91)!

- What sources of worry are outside your boundaries?

- Whom have you been trying to change?

- What can you do to positively influence those people instead of trying to change them?

- And what can you do to change yourself—specifically, your way of dealing with them—so that their destructive patterns no longer work on you?

You need the wisdom to know what is you and what is not you. Pray for the wisdom to know the difference between what you have the power to change and what you do not. Make the serenity prayer your own: "God, grant me the serenity to accept the things I cannot change, the courage to change the things I can, and the wisdom to know the difference" (p. 90).

Law #4: The Law of Respect

When we think about setting boundaries and trying to live by them, we fear that others will not respect them. We focus on others and lose clarity about ourselves (p. 91).

Sometimes the problem is that we judge other people's boundaries. The Bible says whenever we judge, we will be judged (Matt. 7:1–2). When we judge others' boundaries, ours will fall under the same judgment. If we condemn others' boundaries, we can expect them to condemn ours (p. 92).

- Review the list of comments at the bottom of page 91. Which kinds of thoughts—judgments—have you had about other people's boundaries?

- Why does this perspective on other people's boundaries make it difficult to set your own?

- With whom have you been caught up in this fear cycle and therefore been afraid to set the boundaries you need to set? With whom do you comply rather than set boundaries?

This is where the Law of Respect comes in (p. 92).

- Again, what does Jesus teach in Matthew 7:12?

- What does this teaching mean for boundaries?

We need to respect the boundaries of others in order to earn respect for our own. We need to treat their boundaries the way we want them to treat ours (p. 92).

- Whose boundaries do you need to have more respect for?

- To whom do you need to, in the spirit of Jesus, grant the freedom to be himself or herself and different from you (2 Cor. 3:17)?

When we accept other people's freedom, we don't get angry, feel guilty, or withdraw our love when they set boundaries with us. When we accept others' freedom, we are also free (p. 92).

Law #5: The Law of Motivation

Review Stan's story on pages 92–93.

- Where do you see yourself in Stan—in his actions, his ideas, and his motivations?

- Is some of your "doing" and sacrificing motivated not by love, but by fear that you won't be loved if you don't comply? If so, what life experiences taught you that love will be removed if you don't do what someone wants?

- Is some of your "doing" motivated by the fear of anger? Again, what life experiences taught you that saying no will lead to angry confrontations?

Besides the fear that we will lose love and the fear that people will be angry with us, other false motives keep us from setting boundaries (pp. 93–94).

- Which of the following false motives have been behind some of your actions?
  - Fear of loneliness
  - Thinking that to love means always to say yes
  - Thinking that "good" people always say yes
  - Trying to overcome the guilt inside and feel good about yourself
  - Paying back all that you've received

- • Trying to gain people's approval, people who represent parents whose approval was withheld
- • Overidentifying with the other person's loss, and feeling the sadness you think your no would cause them

- • What life experiences and early relationships helped engender these false motives?

We are all called into freedom, and this freedom results in gratitude, an overflowing heart, and love for others. God calls us to love one another, and love is the only true motive for what we do (p. 94).

- • When have you experienced that it truly is more blessed to give than to receive (Acts 20:35)? Be specific about the circumstances and your feelings.

- • In general, do you experience gratitude, an overflowing heart, and love for others when you say yes to requests? If not, what kinds of emotions do you feel instead?

If your giving is not leading to cheer, you need to examine the Law of Motivation, a law that says, "Freedom first, service second." If you serve to get free of your fear, you are doomed to failure. Let God work on the fears, resolve them, and create some healthy boundaries to guard the freedom you were called to (p. 94).

Law #6: The Law of Evaluation

When Jason was faced with the prospect of telling his business partner about responsibilities that he wasn't handling well, he learned the difference between hurting *and* harming *someone (pp. 95–96).*

- Explain the difference between hurting and harming someone.

- When has someone protected his or her boundaries and done something that hurt you? Did that action harm you?

- When have you, like Jason, hesitated to do something out of fear of hurting someone? Would your action have harmed that person?

Jesus refers to following him in the tough situations as "the narrow gate" (Matt. 7:13–14 NASB). It's always easier to travel "the [broad] way ... that leads to destruction," not setting boundaries where we need to.

You need to evaluate the effects of setting boundaries and be responsible to—not for—the other person. Deciding to set boundaries is difficult because it requires decision making and confrontation, which may cause pain to someone you love (p. 96).

- What current circumstances call for you to set boundaries?

- If you set boundaries, what pain or disappointment might you cause someone you love?

- Will that pain harm the person?

We cause pain by making choices that others do not like. We also cause pain by confronting people when they are wrong. But as Ephesians 4:25 teaches, we need to be honest with one another about how we are hurt. If we do not share our anger with one another, bitterness and hatred can set in. Just as iron sharpens iron (Prov. 27:17), we need confrontation and truth from others to grow (pp. 96–97).

- Whom would you like to be able to confront about their wrong actions?

- In a time of prayer, ask God to purify your heart and give you the words to say in love. Jot down those ideas here.

- How would you like to respond to the person you confront if he or she is hurt by the words you speak? Remember that hurting a person does not necessarily mean harming him or her.

- How do you tend to respond when someone confronts you with truth about your wrong behavior?

- How would you like to respond next time?

The Bible says that, if we are wise, we will learn from the admonition of a friend (Prov. 27:6). While that admonition can hurt, it can also help. And it is from this perspective that we need to evaluate the pain our confrontation causes other people. We need to see how this hurt is helpful and sometimes even the best thing we can do for that person and the relationship (p. 97).

Law #7: The Law of Proactivity

Paul points out in various epistles that, as in the physical world, for every action in the spiritual realm of human relationships, there is an equal and opposite reaction (Rom. 4:15; 5:20; 7:5; Eph. 6:4; Col. 3:21) (p. 97).

- When have you seen someone, after years of compliance, go ballistic when their pent-up rage explodes? Maybe that is your story. Share your perspective on this behavior—on its importance, on people's reactions to it, on its freeing impact.

We should herald the emancipation of one who is finally free—but rage can be a sign of immaturity (p. 97).

- Reaction phases are necessary but not sufficient for the establishment of boundaries. What does Galatians 5:13, 15 caution about limiting these reaction phases?

Once you have reacted, it is time to rejoin the human race and establish connections as equals, loving your neighbor as yourself.
Proactive people show you what they love, what they want, what they purpose, and what they stand for—as opposed to those who are known by what they hate, what they don't like, what they stand against, and what they will not do (p. 98).

- Where are you on this continuum? Are your boundaries still more reactive (the latter qualities) than proactive (the former)?

- Where are you channeling your power right now—in angry outbursts of pain and rage, or in acts of responsibility and love?

The ultimate expression of power is love: it is the ability not to express power, but to restrain it. Proactive people are able to "love others as themselves," "die to self," and not "return evil for evil" (p. 98).

- Look again at Jesus' words in Matthew 5:38–40. What example of love does he give here?

- In what relationship(s) is it time for you to move past the reactive to the proactive and begin living out the power of love? Make this a topic of prayer.

Spiritual adulthood calls you to own your reactive period and feelings—and then move on from that stage. A reactive stage is necessary, but it is just a stage (pp. 98–99).

Law #8: The Law of Envy

The New Testament speaks strongly against the envious heart (James 4:2). But what does envy have to do with boundaries? Envy is probably the basest emotion we have. A direct result of the Fall, it was Satan's sin (Isa. 14:14). Envy defines good as "what I do not possess" and hates the good that it has. What is so destructive about this sin is that it guarantees that we will not get what we want and keeps us perpetually insatiable and dissatisfied (p. 99).

- What things do you tend to envy most?

As bad as envy is, we are not saying that it is wrong to want things we do not have. God has said that he will give us the desires of our heart (Ps. 37:4). The problem with envy is that it focuses outside our boundaries onto others (p. 99).

- What truth does Paul set forth in Galatians 6:4? What is the focus we are called to here?

Boundaryless people feel empty and unfulfilled. They look at another's sense of fullness and feel envious. This time and energy needs to be spent on taking responsibility for their lack and doing something about it (pp. 99–100).

- Review the situations listed on page 100 and the contrasting list at the bottom. What did you learn from these examples?

- What is God calling you, through this discussion, to do about what you lack? More specifically, what questions would you do well to ask yourself instead of envying others?

- God says, "You have not because you ask not" (James 4:2). What is this verse calling you to make a topic of prayer?

Your envy should always be a sign to you that something is lacking in your life. When you feel envy, ask God to help you understand what you resent, why you do not have whatever you are envying, and whether you truly need it. Ask him to show you how to get there or grieve what you cannot have and be content with what you do have (p. 101).

Law #9: The Law of Activity

Human beings are responders and initiators. We respond to invitations and push ourselves into life. Many times we have boundary problems because we lack initiative—the God-given ability to propel ourselves into life (p. 101).

- Talk about how easy or difficult it is for you to respond to invitations.

- Comment on how easy or difficult it is for you to take initiative in life.

- Review the parable of the talents in Luke 19:12–27. What kind of people succeed in the story and what kind of person lost out?

In the parable, the one who lost out was passive and inactive. Passivity never pays off. God will match our effort, but he will never do our work for us. That would be an invasion of our boundaries. God wants us to be assertive and active, seeking and knocking on the door of life. God's grace covers failure, but it cannot make up for passivity (p. 102).

The sin that God rebukes is not trying and failing, but failing to try. Passive "shrinking back" is intolerable to God. Instead we are to actively work to preserve our souls. That is the role of boundaries: they define and preserve our property, our soul. And our boundaries can only be created by our being active and aggressive, by our knocking, seeking, and asking (Matt. 7:7–8) (p. 102).

- What does Hebrews 10:38–39 say to you personally?

- In what aspect of your life are you failing to try right now?

- Passivity can become an ally of evil by not pushing against it. When have you seen this truth in someone's life or perhaps experienced it yourself?

- Where is God calling you, through this discussion, to be more active? Where will you begin to knock, seek, and ask? Be specific.

Law #10: The Law of Exposure

A boundary defines where you begin and end. The paramount reason why you need such a line is that you do not exist in a vacuum. You exist in relation to God and others. Your boundaries define you in relation to others. Boundaries are really about relationships and love (pp. 102–103).

The Law of Exposure says that your boundaries need to be made visible to others and communicated to them in relationships. We have many boundary problems because of relational fears (pp. 103–104).

- What do these two passages have to say about the importance of communicating boundaries?
  - Ephesians 4:25–26

  - Ephesians 5:13–14

- With whom do you struggle to communicate your boundaries? Why?

- Review the discussion of secret boundaries (p. 103) and the consequences of keeping them secret. What warning to you personally do you find in these real-life situations?

The biblical mandate is to be honest and be in the light. The light is the only place where we have access to God and other people, and our relational problems can only be solved in relationships. Because of our fears, we may hide aspects of ourselves in the darkness, where the devil has an opportunity (p. 104).

- What aspects of yourself do you hide?

- Can you begin to bring them into the light by making them the focus of a prayer? Let God know which parts of yourself you are afraid to share and ask him to bring into your life someone safe with whom you can gradually begin to share those parts.

- According to David's words in Psalm 51:6, what does God want for us?

God wants a real relationship with us and wants us to have real relationships with each other. A real relationship means that I am in the light with my boundaries and other aspects of myself that are difficult to communicate. Our boundaries are affected by sin, and need to be brought into the light for God to heal them and for others to benefit from them. The path to real love is communicating boundaries openly (p. 104).

A Review

- Which laws had the most to say to you?

- How has your understanding of boundaries changed because of this lesson?

- What is God saying to you through this lesson on the laws of boundaries?

- What have you determined to do as a result of what you've learned in this lesson about God's laws, boundaries, and yourself?

Remember the story of the alien? The good news is that when God brings us out from an alien land, he does not leave us untaught. Just as he rescued his people from the Egyptians, he has probably led you out of captivity. He has been your Redeemer and now, like the children of Israel, you need to learn his principles, practice them, and fight many battles to make them a part of your character. That's what this study is all about (p. 104).

Prayer

Creator and Redeemer God, thank for the wondrous universe you've fashioned and the laws that you've established for its functioning. Thank you, too, that similar laws exist in the spiritual realm as well and that, through this study, I am learning more about those laws that govern relationships and my well-being. Father God, I see how these laws are rooted in your love, in your gracious, forgiving, and unconditional love. I ask therefore that you open my heart that I might learn these laws, practice them, internalize them, and ultimately find freedom in them, your laws of love. I pray in Jesus' name. Amen.

Chapter 4

Common Boundary Myths

One of the definitions of a myth is a fiction that looks like a truth, and many myths have grown up around boundaries. Whatever the source of these myths—your family background, your church or theological foundations, your own misunderstandings—prayerfully investigate the following "sound-like-truths" that you have accepted as fact (p. 107).

Myth #1: If I Set Boundaries, I'm Being Selfish

The number one hallmark of Christians is that we love others (John 13:35). But don't boundaries turn us from other-centeredness to self-centeredness? No! Appropriate boundaries actually increase our ability to care about others (p. 107).

    To understand how people with highly developed limits are the most caring people on earth, let's make a distinction between selfishness *and* stewardship *(p. 108).*

- How do you define *selfishness*?

Selfishness has to do with a fixation on our own wishes and desires to the exclusion of our responsibility to love others. Though having wishes and desires is a God-given trait (Prov. 13:4), we are to keep them in line with healthy goals and responsibilities (p. 108).

- Now explain the difference between needs and wants.

- Mr. Insensitive may desperately need help with the fact that he's a terrible listener. When have you not wanted what you've needed? Give two or three examples.

- Read 2 Corinthians 12:7–10 and Philippians 4:12–13. What wish did Paul have that God denied? What does Paul say about the needs he had that God met?

If you're afraid to set boundaries, remember that God is interested in meeting your needs (Phil. 4:19). He will also fulfill many of your wishes (Ps. 37:4) (p. 108).

Our Needs Are Our Responsibility

Despite the fact that we have God's help, we need to understand that meeting our needs is basically our own job. We can't passively wait for others to take care of us. Even knowing that "it is God who works in [us]" (Phil. 2:13), we are our own responsibility (p. 108).

- What instructions are we given in the following passages?
  - Matthew 7:7

  - Philippians 2:12–13

- What is your attitude toward your needs? Are your needs bad? Selfish? A luxury? Things that God or others should provide for you?

- What does Paul say in 2 Corinthians 5:10 about the fact that our lives are our responsibility?

Stewardship

To understand the importance of setting limits, remember that your life is a gift from God. If our lack of boundaries causes us to mismanage our lives, the Owner has a right to be upset with us. We are to develop our lives, abilities, feelings, thoughts, and behaviors. Our spiritual and emotional growth is God's "interest" on his investment in us. When we say no to people and activities that are harmful to us, we are protecting God's investment (p. 109).

- How do you define *stewardship*?

- What does Christian stewardship have to do with carefully defined boundaries?

- What, then, is the difference between *selfishness* and *stewardship* when it comes to setting boundaries?

Myth #2: Boundaries Are a Sign of Disobedience

Many Christians fear that setting and keeping limits signals rebellion or disobedience. The truth is life-changing: a lack *of boundaries is often a sign of disobedience (p. 109).*

- When have you seen individuals—or when have you yourself been—trapped in activities of no genuine spiritual and emotional value because of this myth?

- Remember Barry (pp. 109—110)? What good thing had Barry done—and for what bad reasons?

- When have you done a good thing for a bad reason? What fear motivated you to say yes when you wanted to say no?

Barry committed himself to a Bible study—out of fear that he would lose relation-ships with people in the singles group if he disappointed Ken. The story of Barry is important, as is the experience you just shared, because it illustrates the biblical principle that an internal no nullifies an external yes. After all, God is more con-cerned about our hearts than he is with our outward compliance (Hos. 6:6). When we say yes to God or anyone else when we really mean no, we move into a position of compliance. And that is the same as lying (p. 110).

- Reflect on the commitment you made with an external yes despite your internal no. Did it become an external no? Did you fulfill your commitment? If so, with what attitude?

- What decision do you currently face? How does this perspective on yes and no help you?

To better understand why it is a myth that boundaries are a sign of disobedience, consider this: If we can't say no, we can't say yes. We must always say yes out of a heart of love. When our motive is fear—of a real person or a guilty conscience—we love not. And God doesn't want us to obey out of fear, but out of love (p. 111).

- According to 2 Corinthians 9:7, what are two unhealthy internal reasons for saying yes and giving of yourself, your talents, your time, or your treasure?

- In the same verse, what does "cheerful" suggest about a healthy internal reason for saying yes?

- "Reluctantly" and "under compulsion" both involve fear. What does 1 John 4:18 say about fear?

- Where are you acting out of fear rather than love? How could this discussion of Myth #2 change your life?

Boundaries can be a sign of disobedience. We can say no to good things for wrong reasons, but having that no—setting that boundary—helps us to clarify, to be honest, and to recognize the truth about our motives. Then we can allow God to work in us (p. 111).

Myth #3: If I Begin Setting Boundaries, I Will Be Hurt by Others

Many people genuinely believe in the necessity of boundaries but are terrified of their consequences. It is possible that others will become angry at our boundaries and attack or, worse, withdraw from us. God never gave us the power or the right to control how others respond to our no (p. 111).

Read the account of Jesus and the rich young ruler in Matthew 19:16–22.

- Understanding that the young man worshiped money, what did Jesus instruct him to do?

- How did the young man respond to Jesus' instruction?

Unable to make room in his heart for God by giving away his wealth, the young man turned and walked away (p. 112).

- What did Jesus do?

Jesus let the ruler go—and we should do no less. We can't manipulate people into swallowing our boundaries by sugarcoating them (p. 112).

Boundaries are a "litmus test" for the quality of our relationships. Those people in our lives who can respect our boundaries will love our wills, our opinions, our separateness. Those who can't respect our boundaries are telling us that they don't love our no. They only love our yes, our compliance (Luke 6:26).

- Whose boundaries do you have trouble respecting? What does the truth in the preceding paragraph teach you about yourself?

- Who has had a difficult time respecting your boundaries when you've tried to establish and live by them? What does their difficulty suggest about that relationship?

The Bible clearly distinguishes between those who love truth and those who don't (p. 112).

- Explain the connection between setting limits and telling the truth.

- Setting boundaries is a way to tell the truth about who you are. When has setting boundaries led to increased intimacy in a relationship?

It's only from a place of being "rooted and grounded in love" (Eph. 3:17 NASB) that you can safely begin learning to tell the truth. Such bonds enable us to set boundaries. And while some people will abandon or attack us for having boundaries, it is better to know about their character so that we can take steps to fix the problem (p. 114).

- With this truth in mind, consider in what relationship you need to establish some boundaries today. What do you feel the risks are? When will you take a bold step of setting limits? Who will be there to support you with prayer?

Myth #4: If I Set Boundaries, I Will Hurt Others

If you fear that setting boundaries will injure someone you care about, the problem is that you are seeing boundaries as an offensive weapon. Nothing could be further from the truth. Boundaries are a defensive *tool (p. 114).*

- When have you seen others use boundaries as an offensive weapon?

- When have you used boundaries as an offensive weapon?

- Explain your understanding of the statement "Boundaries are a defensive tool."

Appropriate boundaries don't control, attack, or hurt anyone. They simply prevent your treasures from being taken at the wrong time. This principle speaks not only to those who would like to control or manipulate us, but it also applies to the legitimate needs of others (p. 114).

- How have you responded when someone has maintained his or her boundaries despite your legitimate needs?

There are times when, for some reason or another, we can't sacrifice. Jesus left the multitudes, for example, to be alone with his Father (Matt. 14:22–23). In these instances, we have to allow others to take responsibility for their burdens (Gal. 6:5) and to look elsewhere to get their needs met (pp. 114–115).

- In light of this (perhaps new) perspective, how do you want to respond—internally and externally—the next time someone maintains appropriate boundaries and leaves you to look elsewhere to get your needs met?

Clearly, we all need more than God and a best friend. We need a group of supportive relationships because having more than one person in our lives allows our friends to be human, to be busy, to be unavailable at times, to hurt and have problems of their own, and to have time alone. In these supportive relationships, we will also learn that other people can tolerate our no. When our supportive network is strong enough, we all help each other mature into what God intended us to be (Eph. 4:2–3). When we've taken the responsibility to develop several supportive relationships, we can take a no from someone and even from God. And God tells us no quite often! He doesn't worry that his boundaries will injure us. He knows we are to take responsibility for our lives—and sometimes a no helps us do just that (p. 115).

- What supportive relationships do you enjoy? If your list isn't much longer than "God and my best friend," where will you go to find others? And when will you take that step?

Myth #5: Boundaries Mean That I am Angry

Quite often, when people begin telling the truth, setting limits, and taking responsibility, an "angry cloud" follows them around for a while (pp. 115–116).

- Why does it make sense that setting limits might put you in touch with some feelings of anger? Consider Brenda's situation or one of your own.

Boundaries don't cause anger in us. Instead, anger—which we may finally notice when we attempt to establish boundaries—is, like all other emotions, a signal. And anger signals danger. Rather than urging us to withdraw (as fear does), anger is a sign that we need to move forward to confront the threat. Anger can tell us that our boundaries have been violated. It can tell us we're in danger of being injured or controlled. It can tell us that we may be demanding something we shouldn't have. Anger also provides us with a sense of power to solve a problem. It energizes us to protect ourselves, those we love, and our principles (p. 116).

- In John 2:13–17, what did Jesus' anger signal? And what did he do in response to the anger he felt?

- How did the family you grew up in deal with anger? What models did you have for what to do with anger?

- Do you let yourself experience anger? Why or why not? If you do, how do you deal with it?

- Explain how anger can be an ally.

- When has anger energized you to confront someone or set a limit? Be specific about what you were protecting or the problem you were solving.

As with all emotions, anger doesn't understand time. Anger doesn't dissipate auto-matically. It has to be worked through appropriately. Otherwise, anger simply lives inside the heart. Like a servant who becomes king, old anger can be a real tyrant for a time (Prov. 30:22), but you don't have to remain angry forever (p. 117).

- Are you aware of "old anger" inside your heart? If so, what are you doing to work through it appropriately?

The first step toward resolving past anger is to experience the grace of God through others who will love you in your anger (p. 118).

- In what relationship(s) can you confess your anger from the past, as the Bible calls us to do (James 5:16)?

The second step is to rebuild the injured parts of your soul (p. 118).

- What are you doing to take responsibility for healing "treasures" that have been violated?

Finally, as you develop a sense of biblical boundaries, you find more safety in the present. You are more confident and less enslaved to your fear of others (pp. 118–119).

- Do you sense that you are progressing along this continuum? Are you aware of a new feeling of safety, a new sense of confidence, or a new freedom from fear of others beginning to take root? What are you doing to encourage its growth?

Don't fear the rage you discover when you first begin developing boundaries. It is the protest of earlier parts of your soul, parts that need to be unveiled, understood, and loved by God and people. Then you need to take responsibility for healing them and for developing better boundaries than anger (p. 119).

Individuals with mature boundaries are the least angry people in the world. Because they prevent boundary violation in the first place, they are more in control of their lives and values, and don't need anger (p. 119).

- Where have you seen an example of this in real life? Whom do you know who lives by clearly defined boundaries? How angry is this person?

Myth #6: When Others Set Boundaries, It Injures Me

Since being on the receiving end of boundaries is hurtful, we may vow never to hurt someone else by maintaining our boundaries. Let's consider why accepting others' boundaries is such a problem (p. 120).

- First, having inappropriate boundaries set on us can injure us, especially in childhood. What inappropriate boundaries, if any, have injured you? Be specific.

- Second, we project our own injuries onto others. In what relationship(s) may you be reading your pain in other people?

- Third, an inability to receive someone's boundary may mean there is an idolatrous relationship. Whose boundaries—whose no—do you have an especially hard time accepting? Are you putting that person on the throne that should only be occupied by God?

- Fourth, an inability to accept others' boundaries can indicate a problem in taking responsibility. Are you so accustomed to others rescuing you that you have begun to believe that your well-being is someone else's problem? In other words, are you failing to take responsibility for your own life?

In a letter that has since been lost, Paul set limits on the Corinthians' rebelliousness (p. 122).

- According to 2 Corinthians 7:8–9, how did the Corinthians respond to the limits Paul set?

- Describe a situation in your life where setting boundaries—either you setting boundaries for yourself or someone maintaining their boundaries in their relationship with you—could lead to repentance.

In Matthew 7:12, Jesus shares that Golden Rule: "In everything, do to others what you would have them do to you."

- What does this rule say to you about boundaries?

Do you want others to respect your boundaries? Then you must be willing to respect the boundaries of others (p. 122).

Myth #7: Boundaries Cause Feelings of Guilt

One of the major obstacles to setting boundaries is our feeling of obligation. What do we owe our parents, friends, and anyone else who has been loving toward us? What is appropriate and biblical, and what is not (p. 123)?

Many people solve this dilemma by avoiding setting boundaries with those to whom they feel an obligation. Sometimes moving on from a church, a job, or a friend would be a mature move, but feelings of obligation keep us from doing so (p. 123).

- Where have feelings of obligation prevented you from setting boundaries?

- What have been the consequences of your failure to set boundaries in the situation(s) you listed? Are you, for instance, stuck at home, in a school, in a church, in a job, or in a friendship?

We often think that because we have received something, we owe something. The problem is the nonexistent debt. The love—or money or time—we receive should be accepted as a gift (p. 123).

- What does the word "gift" imply? Asked differently, what is an appropriate response to a gift?

All that's really needed in response to a gift is gratitude. The giver has no thought that the present will provide a return. It was simply provided because someone loved someone and wanted to do something for him or her. Period (p. 123).

- God's gift of salvation to us cost him his Son. It was a gift motivated out of his love for us (John 3:16). Our response to God's gift is to receive it and be grateful. According to 2 Corinthians 9:6, 7 and Colossians 2:7, why is our gratitude so important to God?

God knows that our gratitude for what he has done for us will move us to love others (p. 123).

- We owe thanks to God and others who have given to us. Then, from a grateful heart, we should go out and help others. Where are you reaching out to others in grateful response to what you have received from God and his people?

As his Revelation letters to the churches of Ephesus, Pergamum, and Thyatira il-lustrate, God doesn't allow gratitude and boundaries to be confused. Although he is grateful to the churches and praises their accomplishments for the kingdom, he sets boundaries with them by confronting their irresponsibilities (p. 124).

- Through this discussion, what relationship is God calling you to set boundaries in, despite what that person has given you?

God doesn't allow the issues of gratitude and boundaries to be confused, and nei-ther should we. Our feelings of gratitude shouldn't keep us from setting boundaries with those who have given gifts to us (p. 124).

Myth #8: Boundaries Are Permanent, and I'm Afraid of Burning My Bridges

It's important to understand that your no is always subject to you. You own your boundaries, they don't own you. If you set limits with someone and he or she responds maturely and lovingly, you can renegotiate the boundary. In addition, you can change the boundary when you are in a safer place. The Bible shows us many instances when boundaries were renegotiated and changed (Jonah 3:10; Acts 15:37–39; 2 Tim. 4:11) (p. 124).

- What boundary or boundaries have you failed to set out of fear that it would be permanent?

- Have you ever been aware of someone changing boundaries with you? Talk about the specifics—what changes were made, how they were made, and how you responded.

- What boundaries are you more willing to set now that you know they needn't be permanent?

A Review

- Which myths have you accepted as truth?

- How has your understanding of boundaries changed because of this lesson?

- What is God saying to you through this lesson on boundary myths?

- What have you determined to do as a result of what you've learned here about God's truth, boundaries, and yourself?

As we did at the beginning of this lesson, we again encourage you to prayerfully review those myths that have entangled and ensnared you. Search the Scriptures mentioned in the text and this guide. Ask God to give you a sense of confidence that he believes in good boundaries more than you do.

Prayer

Gracious and good Father, you have promised that your truth shall set us free, and I thank you for the truths of this lesson. I've had a glimpse of the freedom that comes with boundaries and with understanding boundaries. I ask now that you would help these truths — your truths — penetrate my heart. Help me to change my wrong assumptions and beliefs. Free me from false thinking and guide my actions. I continue to ask you to teach me to set boundaries. Please help me to do so wisely and always in love. I pray in your Son's name. Amen.

Part Two

Boundary Conflicts

--- *Chapter 5* ---

Boundaries and Your Family

Having asked and answered the question, "What are boundaries?" we now move on to Part Two and a study of boundary conflicts. The first area of conflict we'll look at is the family.

A Common Problem

Susie suffered a deep depression after returning from a visit to her parents' home. She felt as if she were bad for living where she lived and had a nagging sense that she really should do what her parents wanted her to do. She had made choices on the outside—she'd moved away, pursued a career, gotten married, had a child—but on the inside things were different. She did not have emotional permission to be a separate person and make free choices about her life without feeling guilty when she did not do what her parents wanted (pp. 129–130).

- How do you feel when you are visiting your parents' home? How do you feel after you return to your own home?

- What choices have you made that your parents have let you know, in one way or another, that they don't fully approve of?

- Have you made these choices on the inside as well as the outside? Or do you feel guilty, apologetic, or uneasy about your choices?

People who own their lives do not feel guilty when they make choices about where they are going (Josh. 24:15). They take other people into consideration, but when they make choices for the wishes of others, they are choosing out of love, not guilt; to advance a good, not to avoid being bad (2 Cor. 9:6–7) (p. 130).

- Do you feel guilty about certain choices that you have made? If so, which ones—and why do you feel guilty? Do you not really "own" yourself?

- What guides the decisions you make? Do you choose out of love or guilt? Do you choose to advance a good or to avoid being bad? Give specific examples and be honest with yourself about your motives.

Signs of a Lack of Boundaries

Let's look at some common signs of a lack of boundaries with the family you grew up in.

Catching the Virus

When we don't have good boundaries, our family of origin has the power to affect our new family. In fact, one sure sign of boundary problems is when your relationship with one person has the power to affect your relationships with others (pp. 130–131).

- Does the description of Susie remind you of someone you know, someone who is giving one person way too much power in his or her life? Be specific about who that person is and the evidence that someone in his or her family of origin has too much power.

- Are you like Susie? If so, be specific about the person who affects your relationships with others. How do you respond emotionally to that person? What is the emotional fallout from contact with that person?

- How does that fallout impact your feelings about yourself? Your other relationships?

Second Fiddle

Another common sign of a lack of boundaries with the family of origin is when the spouse feels like he or she gets the leftovers. Dan feels that Jane's real allegiance is to her parents rather than to him, her husband. Jane didn't complete the "leaving" before she tried the "cleaving" aspect of marriage (Gen. 2:24). For marriage to work, spouses need to loosen their ties with their families of origin and forge new ones with the family being created by marriage (p. 131).

- If you are married, are you pleased with the boundaries your spouse maintains with his or her family of origin—or do you feel like you get leftovers? Support your answer with specific examples.

- Do you think your spouse is pleased with the boundaries you maintain with your family of origin? Ask him or her.

- Where do you need to loosen ties with your family of origin? What specific steps will you take to strengthen ties or forge new ones with the family that was created by your marriage?

May I Have My Allowance, Please?

Remember the description of Terry and Sherry's life? He could not set boundaries on his parents' desire for him and Sherry to have certain material things. Although his parents' handouts cut into Terry's self-respect, he wasn't sure he wanted to forsake them for a greater sense of independence. He was not yet an adult financially (p. 132).

- Are you an adult financially? Support your answer with specific details about your life.

The financial boundary problem can take another tack: Parents may continue to finance the road of failure and irresponsibility when they help their children out of financial messes caused by drug or alcohol use, out-of-control spending, or the modern "I haven't found my niche" syndrome (p. 132).

- When have you seen—or perhaps even experienced—this kind of financial boundary problem?

- How well do you live within your means and pay for your own failures? Are you an adult financially? Are your boundaries clearly defined and carefully maintained when it comes to your finances and your parents?

Mom, Where Are My Socks?

In the perpetual child syndrome, a person may be financially on his own, but allow his family of origin to perform certain life management functions (p. 133).

- What, if any, life management functions are you still allowing your parents to perform for you?

- If you are allowing your parents to perform life management functions for you, your other adult relationships may be dysfunctional. Evaluate those relationships. Have you chosen "black sheep"? Are you unable to commit to a member of the opposite sex or to a career?

- How are your finances? Do they reflect your ability to consider and plan for the future? Or is yours an essentially adolescent financial life, reflecting no thought beyond the immediate present?

Three's a Crowd

Dysfunctional families are known for a certain type of boundary problem called triangulation, a term that refers to the failure to resolve a conflict between two persons and the pulling in of a third to take sides. The third person has no business in the conflict but is used for comfort and validation by the ones who are afraid to confront each other. In a triangle, people speak falsely. Failing to own their anger, they cover it up with nice words and flattery. Gossip further erodes the relationships of the parties involved (Eph. 4:25) (pp. 133–135).

• When have you been involved in a triangle like this? Were you Person A, Person B, or Person C? If triangulation is the mode for your family, which person do you tend to be?

• What did your family of origin teach you about resolving conflict and dealing with anger?

• What does the Bible teach in the following passages?
  • Leviticus 19:17

  • Proverbs 28:23

  • Matthew 5:23–24

  • Matthew 18:15

We can avoid triangulation by talking to the person with whom we have a conflict. Never say to a third party something about someone that you do not plan to say to the person himself (p. 135).

- What conflict do you need to resolve directly right now?

Who's the Child Here, Anyhow?

Early in life, some people learned that they were responsible for their parents, who were stuck in childish patterns of irresponsibility. Every time they tried to have separate lives, they felt selfish (pp. 135–136).

- Do you feel responsible for your parents? Is it unhealthy or is it a biblical, healthy responsibility?

The Bible teaches that adult children should help care for their elderly parents (1 Tim. 5:3–4). It is good to feel grateful to our parents and to repay them for what they have done for us (p. 136). But there are two problems that sometimes crop up.

- Are you at the point of needing to care for elderly parents? If so, are you facing either of these problems?
  - Do you have parents who aren't really in need but are acting like martyrs or being demanding?

  - Do you find yourself lacking the clear boundaries you need to determine what you can give and what you can't give?

- Explain why "good boundaries prevent resentment" and then, perhaps by taking a reading of your own level of resentment, evaluate the boundaries you have set or are resetting with your parents. Or are you reacting by not giving to your parents at all?

But I'm Your Brother

Another frequent dynamic is an irresponsible adult child depending on a responsible adult sibling (p. 136).

- Do you see this happening in your family of origin? If so, where and what role, if any, are you playing?

- Why can a needy sibling tear down our best-built fences?

- Review the signs of a lack of boundaries and comment on the condition of your boundaries with your family of origin. Where are the boundaries doing the job? Where could they be more clearly defined or more strongly maintained?

But Why Do We Do That?

Why in the world do we choose to continue the sorts of family patterns we've just looked at? Let's look at two reasons (pp. 136–138).

Continuation of Old Boundary Problems

One reason why these unhealthy patterns continue is that we did not learn the laws of boundaries in our family of origin. Our adult boundary problems are actually old boundary problems that have been there since childhood (p. 137).

- Which of the following patterns that you learned while growing up are continuing into adulthood with the same players?
  - Lack of consequences for irresponsible behavior
  - Lack of confrontation
  - Lack of limits
  - Taking responsibility for others instead of yourself
  - Giving out of compulsion and resentment
  - Envy
  - Passivity
  - Secrecy
- Since you can recognize the struggles you are having with boundaries in your family of origin, now identify which laws of boundaries are being broken (chapter five in the text) and list them below.

- What negative fruit is resulting in your life as a result of the laws you just listed as being broken?

The patterns you've identified run deep. The family members who taught you how to organize your life may send you back to old patterns by their very presence. You begin to act out of memory rather than growth. To change, you must confess these "sins of the family," repent of them, and change the way you handle them (Ex. 20:5; Neh. 9:2). You've just taken some steps toward doing exactly that (p. 137).

Adoption

Another reason why boundary problems with our family members may continue is that we may not have gone through the biblical transition into adulthood and the spiritual adoption into the family of God (Matt. 23:9; Gal. 4:1–7) (pp. 137–138).

- Are you still holding an allegiance to your earthly parents or have you fully become part of God's family and are now obeying his ways? Give specific evidence supporting your answer.

- Sometimes obeying God's ways can cause conflict in—and even separation from—our families (Matt. 10:35–37), but Jesus teaches that our spiritual ties are the most important (Matt. 12:46–50). Have you experienced conflict in your family of origin because of your obedience and loyalty to Christ? Have you needed to separate from your family of origin? If you answered yes to either question, reflect on how God has guided you and is holding you up.

In the family of God, we are to tell the truth, set limits, take and require responsibility, confront each other, forgive each other, and so on. Such strong standards and values make this family run, and God will not condone any other behaviors in his family (p. 138).

Becoming part of God's family in no way means that we are to cut other ties. We are to have friends outside of God's family and strong ties with our family of origin. We do, however, need to ask two questions (p. 138).

- Do any of your ties to your family of origin or to friends outside of God's family keep you from doing the right thing in some situations? List those people's names and describe the kind and the extent of their influence over you.

- Have you really become an adult in relation to your family of origin? If so, give specific examples of your adult behavior. If not, list some situations in which you don't feel you acted or were treated like an adult. Comment on why you think you are unable to fully mature.

If our ties to our family of origin are truly loving, we will be separate and free, able to give out of love and a "purposeful" heart. We will stay away from resentment, we will love with limits, and we will not enable evil behavior (p. 138).

- List the members of your family of origin and evaluate your relationship with each of them. Are you separate? Free? Do you give out of love and a "purposeful" heart (2 Cor. 9:6–7)? Do you avoid feeling resentful? Do you love with limits? Do you keep from enabling evil behavior?

If we are not "under guardians and managers" as adults, we can make truly adult decisions, having control over our own will (1 Cor. 7:37), subject to our true Father (p. 138).

Resolution of Boundary Problems with Family

Establishing boundaries with families of origin is a tough task, but one with great reward. It is a process, with certain distinguishable steps (p. 139).

Identify the Symptom

Take a moment to consider your own life situation.

- Where do boundary problems exist with your parents and/or your siblings?

- Where have you lost control of your property?

- What connection do you see between the areas where you have lost control and the family you grew up in?

Identify the Conflict

Now discover what dynamic is being played out. You cannot stop acting out a dynamic until you understand what you are doing. "Take the plank out" of your own eye and find your boundary violations (Matt. 7:1–5) (p. 139).

- What laws of boundaries are you violating? Do you triangulate? Do you take responsibility *for* a sibling or parent instead of being responsible *to* them? Do you fail to enforce consequences and end up paying for their behavior? Are you passive and reactive toward them and the conflict?

Identify the Need That Drives the Conflict

You do not act in inappropriate ways for no reason. You are often trying to meet some underlying need that your family of origin did not meet. Face this deficit and accept that it can only be met in your new family of God, those who do God's will and can love you the way he designed (p. 139).

- What needs did your family of origin not meet for you? Your need, for instance, to be loved? Approved of? Accepted? Understood? Free to be yourself?

Take in and Receive the Good

It is not enough to understand your need. You must get it met. God is willing to meet your needs through his people, but you must humble yourself, reach out to a good support system, and take in the good. With God at your side, learn to respond to and receive love (2 Cor. 6:11–13)—and it's okay if you're clumsy at first (pp. 139–140).

- How strong is your support system? Is there one person with whom you can begin to share what you're learning about yourself, your needs, and your plans to establish better boundaries (see Eccl. 4:9–12)?

- Why do you hesitate to reach out to people through whom God can meet your needs? Let God know of your concerns and anxieties, and listen for his reminder that he will be with you as you reach out.

- What good would you like to be able to take in? Again, tell God about your struggle (after all, he already knows!) and remember that he loves you and wants you to receive the good that's available in his family and his world.

Practice Boundary Skills

Your boundary skills are fragile and new. You can't take them immediately into a difficult situation. Practice them in situations where they will be honored and respected. Look at practicing your boundary skills as if it's physical therapy. In both instances, people gradually build up to the heavy stuff (p. 140).

- With whom can you practice saying no? Who will honor your no and continue to love you unconditionally? Be alert for an opportunity to flex this new muscle!

- When you do say no, note how you felt, how the person responded, and what you learned. Talk through the experience with someone you feel safe with so that you can be sure you are on the right track about what you did and why.

Say No to the Bad

In addition to practicing new skills in safe situations, avoid hurtful situations. Avoid those people who have abused and controlled you in the past. When you think you are ready to reestablish a relationship with someone who has been abusive and controlling in the past, you may want to bring a friend or supporter along.

The injury you are recovering from is serious, and you can't reestablish a relationship until you have the proper tools (p. 140).

- What upcoming situations do you know could be hurtful? What will you do instead of putting yourself in those abusive circumstances?

- What people would you do well to avoid as you are developing healthier boundaries? In the past, who has abandoned you or been controlling?

Forgive the Aggressor

Nothing clarifies boundaries more than forgiveness. When you refuse to forgive someone, you still want something from that person, and it keeps you tied to him or her forever. Refusing to forgive a family member is one of the main reasons people are unable to separate from their dysfunctional family. They still want something from them. It is much better to receive grace from God, who has much to give, and to forgive those who have no money to pay their debt with (Matt. 18:21–35) (pp. 140–141).

- Whom are you not forgiving?

- What do you still want from that person? Love? Confession of wrongdoing? An apology? Something else?

Spend a few quiet moments in prayer. Talk to God about your struggle to let go and forgive. Ask him to help you want to forgive. Ask him to teach you to forgive and to help you receive his grace, which can heal the hurts you sustained in your family of origin. When you forgive the aggressor, your suffering ends. The wish for repayment that is never forthcoming—a wish that makes your heart sick because your hope is deferred (Prov. 13:12)—will die, and you will be free (pp. 140–141).

Respond, Don't React

When you respond to what someone says or does, you remain in control, with options and choices. But when you react to what someone says or does, you may have a problem with boundaries. If someone is able to cause havoc by doing or saying something, that person is in control of you, and your boundaries are lost (p. 141).

- Who has been able to cause you to react by doing or saying something? Asked differently, who exercises a good deal of control over you?

If you feel yourself reacting, step away so that family members can't force you to do or say something you don't want to, something that violates your separateness. When you react, the other person is in control. When you respond, you are (Gal. 5:23) (p. 141).

- When, if ever, have you been able to keep your boundaries with someone who has controlled you? What did you do? What did you learn from that experience?

Learn to Love in Freedom and Responsibility, Not in Guilt

Boundaries in no way mean to stop loving. Instead, with boundaries, you gain freedom to love. It is good to sacrifice and deny yourself for the sake of others, but you need boundaries to make that choice (p. 141).

- When have you been motivated more by guilt than love in a family relationship?

- What boundary violations were involved in that guilt-ridden relationship?

The person who has to remain forever in a protective mode is losing out on love and freedom. In fact, the best boundaries are loving ones (p. 1341).

- Where can you practice purposeful giving so that you can experience the freedom that comes with boundaries? Be specific about your plan—and have someone hold you accountable.

As you continue to develop stronger boundaries with your family of origin, remember that doing good for someone, when you freely choose to do it, is boundary enhancing, not codependent (John 13:34–35) (p. 141).

Prayer

Heavenly Father, you designed families as a place for us to learn about you and your love—but families don't always teach us that. You know the dysfunction, the pain, and the untruths we can learn instead. You know the patterns of the family I grew up in, and what I didn't learn about boundaries that I need to learn now. Teach me. Help me to clearly define my boundaries and to do a better job maintaining them. Give me the courage and wisdom to take steps toward resolving my boundary problems with my family. I pray in Jesus' name. Amen.

Chapter 6

Boundaries and Your Friends

The word friendship *conjures up images of intimacy, fondness, and a mutual draw-ing together of two people. Despite their desire to be together, though, friends can still experience boundary conflicts (p. 143).*

A Brief Inventory

In this discussion of boundaries, we define friendship *as a nonromantic relation-ship that is attachment-based rather than function-based. We're looking not at relationships based on a common task, like work or ministry, but friendships in which people simply want to be together (1 John 4:12) (p. 143).*

- What friends come to mind when you read this definition? List them.

- In which, if any, of the relationships you just listed have you felt, like Marsha, as if you're the one always taking the initiative?

- In which of the relationships you listed do you find a real mutuality and comfort?

- What makes one relationship lopsided and another comfortable and easy? Share your ideas before you move on.

As Marsha realized, and as you probably have, boundary conflicts with friends come in all sizes and shapes. To understand the various issues, let's look at four conflicts and how they can be resolved with boundaries. We'll apply a boundary checklist to these to help you locate where you are in setting boundaries and show you how to get where you want to go (p. 143).

Conflict #1: Compliant/Compliant

When two compliants like Sean and Tim interact, neither does what he really wants. Each is so afraid of telling the other the truth that neither ever does (p. 144).

- When, if ever, have you been in a Sean/Tim relationship? Describe how you felt about the friendship and where the friendship stands now.

- Review the boundary checklist on pages 144–145. What do these eight points suggest to you about a healthy step you could take in your compliant/compliant friendship?

- When will you take this step? What supportive relationship(s) will you lean on when you do?

As the two compliants become more open about their likes and dislikes, they may find themselves separating more from each other. They need to remember that having different friends for different activities is no blot on a relationship—and it might even help in the long run (Prov. 18:24) (p. 145).

Conflict #2: Compliant/Aggressive Controller

In a compliant/aggressive controller conflict, the compliant feels intimidated and inferior in the relationship; the aggressive controller feels irritated at being nagged by the compliant (p. 145).

- When, if ever, have you been in a compliant/aggressive controller relationship? Describe how you felt about the friendship and where the friendship stands now.

- Review the boundary checklist on pages 146–147. What do these eight points suggest to you about a healthy step you could take in your compliant/aggressive controller friendship? (Since the compliant is usually the one that is unhappy in this relationship, he or she is the one who needs to take action.)

- When will you take this step? What supportive relationship(s) will you lean on when you do?

When the compliant confronts his aggressive controller friend, he sets limits to let her know that her control hurts him and wounds their friendship. The aggressive controller may feel empathic remorse for the pain she has caused or experience the consequences of her actions and begin to take responsibility for the control that ran her friend off. At this point, if both are willing, the two can renegotiate the relationship and build a new friendship (Prov. 27:17) (p. 147).

Conflict #3: Compliant/Manipulative Controller

A manipulative controller may not be consciously trying to manipulate her friends. However, no matter what her good intentions are, when she's in a jam, she uses them. She takes them for granted, thinking that they shouldn't mind doing a friend a favor. Her friends stifle their resentment (p. 147).

- When, if ever, have you been in a compliant/manipulative controller relationship? Describe how you felt about the friendship and where the friendship stands now.

- Review the boundary checklist on pages 147–149. What do these eight points suggest to you about a healthy step you could take in your compliant/manipulative controller friendship? (Again, since the compliant is the unhappy party, he or she is the one who needs to take action.)

- When will you take this step? What supportive relationship(s) will you lean on when you do?

When the compliant feels strong enough, she confronts the manipulative controller, tells about feeling used and taken advantage of, and explains that she wants a more mutual friendship. The manipulative controller, unaware of how she was hurting her friend, may be genuinely sorry and has the option to begin taking more responsibility. The friendship can then grow and deepen (Prov. 10:18) (pp. 148–149).

Conflict #4: Compliant/Nonresponsive

In a compliant/nonresponsive conflict, one friend does all the work while the other coasts along. One party feels frustrated and resentful; the other wonders what the problem is (p. 149).

- When, if ever, have you been in a compliant/nonresponsive relationship? Describe how you felt about the friendship and where the friendship stands now.

- Review the boundary checklist on pages 149–150. What do these eight points suggest to you about a healthy step you could take in your compliant/manipulative controller friendship? (Again, since the compliant is the unhappy party, he or she is the one who needs to take action.)

- When will you take this step? What supportive relationship(s) will you lean on when you do?

The compliant begins to set boundaries by telling the nonresponsive about her feelings and informing her that she will need to take equal responsibility for the friendship in the future. The compliant hopes that the nonresponsive will call, but if the unresponsiveness continues, the compliant has learned it wasn't a mutual connection. Now she can grieve, get over it, and make a choice. This kind of confrontation either exposes the friendship as a one-sided relationship or provides a foundation for rebuilding a better one (Gal. 6:5) (p. 150).

Questions about Friendship Boundary Conflicts

People who are caught in the conflicts we've just looked at often raise the following questions when they consider setting boundaries in their friendships (p. 150).

Question #1: Aren't Friendships Easily Broken?

Most friendships have no external commitment, such as marriage, work, or church, to keep the friends together. So aren't friendships at great risk of breaking up when boundary conflicts arise (pp. 150–151)?

- First, realize that external institutions such as marriage, work, and church are not the only glue that holds relationships together. What evidence of this do you see in the world around you?

- What does Romans 7:19 suggest about trying to base a friendship on commitment only?

Even when we commit to a loving friendship, bad things happen. We let friends down. Feelings go sour. Simply white-knuckling it won't reestablish the relationship. As we stay connected to God, to our friends, and to our support groups, we are filled with the grace to hang in there and fight out the boundary conflicts that arise (p. 151).

- What do Romans 8:1 and Ephesians 4:32 suggest about a strong basis for a friendship?

- When has being "in Christ Jesus" strengthened one of your friendships? When, for instance, has it helped you weather the storm of disappointment, hurt, or even betrayal? Be specific.

- The Bible teaches that all commitment is based on a loving relationship. Being loved leads to commitment and willful decision-making—not the reverse. What is your commitment to God based on? How did first being loved by God lead to your commitment to him (1 John 4:19)?

- What does the truth that "all commitment is based on a loving relationship" say to you personally about friendships?

All friendships need to be based on attachment rather than some kind of obligation, or they have a shaky foundation. An attachment rooted in Christ's love is the strongest of all (p. 152).

- The second problem with thinking that friendships are weaker than institution-alized relationships such as marriage, church, and work is in assuming that those aren't attachment-based. What evidence do you see in the world around you that attachment is key to marriage, church, and work relationships? Consider the divorce rate, patterns of church attendance, and attitudes toward work.

- What keeps you connected to your friends? Their performance? Their lovability? Your guilt? Your sense of obligation? Something else?

It's frightening to realize that the only thing holding our friends to us isn't our per-formance, or our lovability, or their guilt, or their obligation. The only thing that will keep them calling, spending time with us, and putting up with us is love. And that's the one thing we can't control (p. 152).

- What are you doing to learn to trust that love over which you have no control? Who is helping you learn how strong a bond the love of a friend can be?

- Who are you helping to learn how strong the bond of love between friends can be?

- What are you doing to strengthen the bond of love?

As we enter more and more into an attachment-based life, we learn to trust love (1 John 4:18). We learn that the bonds of a true friendship are not easily broken.

And we learn that, in a good relationship, we can set limits that will strengthen, not injure, the connection (p. 152).

Question #2: How Can I Set Boundaries in Romantic Friendships?

Single Christians have tremendous struggles with learning to be truth-tellers and limit-setters in romantic, dating friendships. Most of the conflicts revolve around the fear of losing the relationship (p. 152).

• How well do you tell the truth and set limits in your dating friendships?

Dating is a means to find out what kind of person we complement and with whom we are spiritually and emotionally compatible. This fact causes a built-in conflict. When we date, we have the freedom to say, at any time, "This isn't working out" and end the relationship. The other person has the same freedom (pp. 152–153).

• Because of this dynamic, it is best to learn the skill of setting boundaries in non-romantic arenas. Where are you practicing the skill of setting boundaries? What are you learning that you will be able to apply to dating?

Once we've learned to recognize, set, and keep our biblical boundaries, we can use them in dating. Setting limits and telling the truth in romance is necessary to help each person know where he starts and the other person stops (Prov. 4:23) (pp. 153–154).

• How well do you know the boundaries of the person you are dating? Can that person, for instance, say no?

• And how well does he or she know your boundaries? Can he or she hear and receive your no?

- Where do you and the person you're dating disagree?

- When do you have difficulty saying no?

Question #3: What If My Closest Friends Are My Family?

People who don't think they need an intimate circle of friends besides their own parents and siblings misunderstand the biblical function of the family (p. 154).

- How would you describe the job of a family? What do you think God intends to have happen in our family of origin?

God intends the family to be an incubator in which we grow the maturity, tools, and abilities we need in the outside world. We are then to leave that incubator (Gen. 2:24) and establish a spiritual and emotional family system of our own. Family can indeed be friends, but if you have never questioned, set boundaries, or experienced conflict with your family members, you may not have an adult-to-adult connection with them (John 2:3–4) (p. 154).

- Have you left the incubator of your family? Are you free—do you feel free—to do whatever God has designed for you? Are you spreading God's love to the world and making disciples of other people, thereby accomplishing his purposes for you (Matt. 28:19-20)?

- If you can answer yes to the preceding questions, answer these two as well. What limits have you set with your family of origin? Having left your family, where are you cleaving?

- If you have no "best friends" other than your family, what do you think may be keeping you from separating and individuating? Could it be that you are afraid of becoming an autonomous adult? If so, with whom will you explore those fears?

- If you haven't left your family, what is a limit you can start working on setting?

Question #4: How Can I Set Limits with Needy Friends?

The woman described in this section found that setting limits with friends seemed impossible because they all seemed to be in perpetual crisis. As we talked, we learned that she had never considered the difference between ministries and friendships. This woman's concept of friendship was to find people with needs and throw herself into a relationship with them. She didn't know how to ask for things for herself, which is an act of humility (James 4:2) (p. 155).

- Do you approach friendships as ministries—or do you know someone who does? Explain what this approach to friendship looks like.

- In what relationship(s) have you been the minister, the rescuer, the strong one without needs? Why do you think you chose that role for yourself?

- In what relationship(s) have you been able to ask for things for yourself? What did you ask for and receive?

- If you don't yet feel comfortable asking for things you need, find a safe relationship where you can learn and practice this skill.

When the Bible tells us to comfort with the comfort with which we are comforted (2 Cor. 1:4), it's telling us that we need to be comforted before we can comfort others. That may mean setting boundaries on our ministries so that we can be nurtured by our friends (p. 155).

- What is God saying to you personally through this lesson about boundaries, ministries, and nurturing friendships? And what will you do in response?

Take a prayerful look at your friendships. Ask God to help you determine whether you need to begin building boundaries with some of your friends. Setting boundaries can strengthen friendships, guide your dating life, and serve you well in marriage, the most intimate of human relationships (p. 156).

Prayer

God, it is frightening to me to realize that the only cord tying relationships together is the attachment itself. It's frightening to realize that my friends aren't my friends because of my performance, my lovability, their guilt, or their obligation; that they are my friends because of love — something I can't control. Teach me to trust love — your love and my friends' love. Teach me to love my friends the way I want to be loved — with the unconditional and grace-filled love that you offer us. I pray in the name of Jesus, your Son, my Savior, and the ultimate gift of your love and grace. Amen.

Chapter 7

Boundaries and Your Spouse

If there were ever a relationship where boundaries could get confused, it is mar-riage, where by design husband and wife "become one flesh" (Eph. 5:31). Bound-aries foster separateness. Marriage has as one of its goals the giving up of some of our separateness and becoming one. What a potential state of confusion! And, in fact, more marriages fail because of poor boundaries than any other reason. This chapter applies the laws of boundaries, as well as the boundary myths, to the marital relationship.

Is This Yours, Mine, or Ours?

A marriage mirrors the relationship that Christ has with his bride, the church (Eph. 5:22–33). Christ has some things that only he can do, the church has some things that only it can do, and they have some things they do together (p. 157).

Similarly, in marriage, some duties one spouse does, some the other does, and some they do together (p. 157).

• What are some duties you do?

• What are some duties your spouse does?

- And what are some duties you do together?

- How well is this division of labor working for you and your spouse?

When two people marry, each participates in the relationship, doing duties that correspond to individual abilities and interests, and each has his or her own life. Where boundaries get confused is in the elements of personhood—the elements of the soul that each person possesses and can choose to share with someone else. The problem arises when one trespasses on the other's personhood and tries to control the feelings, attitudes, behaviors, choices, and values of the other (pp. 157–158).

Feelings

One of the most important elements that promotes intimacy between two people is the ability of each to take responsibility for his or her own feelings. We do not communicate our feelings by saying, "I feel that you ..." We communicate our feelings by saying, "I feel sad, or hurt, or lonely, or scared ..." Such vulnerability is the beginning of intimacy and caring (2 Cor. 6:13) (pp. 158–159).

- What feelings are you able to express in your marriage?

- What feelings would you like to be able to express?

- What do you tend to do rather than express your feelings to your spouse?

- How does the behavior you just described affect your relationship with your spouse?

- What feelings do you need to take responsibility for today and share with your spouse?

Desires

Like feelings, desires are another element of personhood that each spouse needs to clarify and take responsibility for. Problems arise when we make someone else responsible for our needs and wants and blame them for our disappointments (James 4:26). Marriage is about getting conflicting wants worked out (pp. 159–160).

- Taking responsibility for getting your wants fulfilled is a rule of life. Review Susan and Jim's situation. What situation in your marriage, if any, does it remind you of?

- What conflicting wants do you and your spouse need to work out?

Limits on What I Can Give

We are finite creatures and must give as we have "decided in [our] heart to give" (2 Cor. 9:7), being aware of when we have given past the love point to the resentment point. Problems arise when we blame our spouse for our own lack of limits. Your spouse is not responsible for your limits; you are. Only you know what you can and want to give, and only you can be responsible for drawing that line. If you do not draw it, you can quickly become resentful (pp. 160–161).

- Often spouses will do more than they really want to and then resent the other for not stopping them from overgiving. Review Bob and Nancy's situation. What situation in your marriage, if any, does it remind you of?

- Where do you need to set some limits on what you will give your spouse?

- Where do you need to take responsibility for your own wants instead of expecting your spouse to take care of them all for you?

Applying the Laws of Boundaries to Marriage

In chapter 5 of the text, we talked about the ten laws of boundaries. Let's apply five of them to troubled marital situations (p. 162).

The Law of Sowing and Reaping

Many times one spouse may be out of control but may not suffer the consequences of this behavior. Letting your spouse suffer the consequences—or being allowed to suffer the consequences for your own behavior—is not manipulation. Instead, someone is limiting how they will allow themselves to be treated and exhibiting self-control. The natural consequences are falling on the shoulders of the responsible party (Gal. 6:7) (pp. 162–163).

- For which of your actions is your spouse not letting you suffer the consequences?

- For which actions do you need to let your spouse suffer the consequences?

- What is keeping you from letting your spouse suffer the consequences for his or her behavior?

The Law of Responsibility

People who set limits exhibit self-control and show responsibility for themselves. Setting limits is an act of love; by binding and limiting the evil, they protect the good. Instead of taking responsibility for people we love, or rescuing them, we need to show responsibility to them by confronting evil when we see it. Keep in mind that the most responsible behavior possible is usually the most difficult (p. 163).

- Where are you getting angry, pouting, and acting disappointed in hopes of controlling your spouse? Where are you waiting to be rescued rather than taking responsibility for yourself?

- Where are you giving in to your spouse's anger, pouting, and disappointments and thereby taking responsibility for what he or she is feeling? Where are you rescuing your spouse (see Prov. 19:19)?

- Explain the difference between being responsible *to* your spouse and being responsible *for* him or her.

- Where do you need to show responsibility in your marriage today? What evil do you see and need to confront?

The Law of Power

We have acknowledged our basic inability to change other people. A better path than nagging, therefore, is accepting people as they are, respecting their choice to be that way, and then letting them experience appropriate consequences. You only have power over yourself. Give up trying to have control and power over someone else (Gal. 5:23) (p. 164).

- What issues do you find yourself nagging your spouse about?

- What do you think about the better path proposed above? What consequences might your spouse experience? Could these consequences prompt the change that your nagging won't?

- Review the "Before Boundaries" and "After Boundaries" examples on page 164. How will you approach your spouse's behavior (the one you've been nagging about) the next time the occasion arises? Plan the words you will say to set boundaries.

- What issues do you find yourself being nagged about? What does this discussion suggest about why you aren't changing? If your spouse were to establish some healthy boundaries, what consequences do you think would prompt a change?

The Law of Evaluation

When you confront your husband or wife and begin to set boundaries, your partner may be hurt. In evaluating the pain that your boundary setting causes your spouse, remember that love and limits go together (Heb. 12:11). When you set boundaries, be lovingly responsible to the person in pain (pp. 164–165).

- How do you think your spouse will react when you start setting boundaries? (Wise and loving spouses accept boundaries and act responsibly toward them. Spouses who are controlling and self-centered will react angrily.) How do you want to respond to the reaction you anticipate?

- You may have already begun setting boundaries. If so, how did your spouse react? And how did you respond to him or her? How would you have liked to respond?

Remember that a boundary always deals with you. You are not demanding that your spouse do anything—even respect your boundaries. You are setting boundaries to say what you will do or will not do (p. 165).

- Keep this truth in mind as you consider your spouse's boundaries. What boundaries of his or hers do you need to respect more?

- And which of your behaviors will that force you to become responsible for?

The Law of Exposure

In a marriage, more so than in any other relationship, the need for revealing boundaries is important. Passive boundaries, such as withdrawal, triangulation, pouting, affairs, and passive-aggressive behavior, are extremely destructive to the relationship (p. 165).

- Where are you or your spouse passively and therefore destructively revealing your boundaries? Look at some of the options listed in the preceding paragraph.

Boundaries need to be communicated first verbally and then with actions. You need to be clear and unapologetic. And the various boundaries we've looked at need to be respected and revealed at different times in marriage (pp. 165–167).

- **Skin:** Physical boundary violations can range from hurtful displays of affection to physical abuse. Where are you not treating your spouse the way you want to be treated? Where is your spouse not treating you the way you want to be treated? What will you say to define the boundary you want him or her to honor?

- **Words:** What issue(s) are you hesitating to confront your spouse about? Where do you need to say, "I do not feel comfortable with that," "I do not want to," or "I won't"? How do you want to respond when your spouse makes statements like those to you?

- **Truth:** Where are you being less than honest in your communication with your spouse? Do you need to tell your partner that he or she is violating one of God's standards (Eph. 4:25)? Do you need to work on owning your feelings and hurts and, in love, communicating those feelings to your spouse?

- **Physical Space:** Do you remove yourself from injurious situations in the marriage to protect your treasures? When you need time away, do you let your spouse know that he or she is experiencing the consequences of his or her out-of-control behavior (Matt. 18:17; 1 Cor. 5:9–13)? Or do you let your partner guess? How would you want your partner to treat you if the roles were reversed? What will you say the next time you need some space?

- **Emotional Distance:** If you have been hurt in a troubled marriage, waiting to trust again is wise. You need to see if your spouse is truly repentant, and you need to judge actions, not mere words (James 2:14–26). Who is praying with you and supporting you as you wait?

- **Time:** Are you giving your spouse the time he or she needs to take care of himself or herself responsibly? Are you taking time for yourself? What do you do apart from your spouse that energizes you and gives you something to bring back to your marriage? Do you take time apart or away from problem areas?

- **Other People:** If you are learning to set boundaries in your marriage, from whom are you getting the help and support your need? If you haven't yet found a counselor or support group, when will you? What is holding you back?

- **Consequences:** What consequences do you need to let your spouse experience? What consequences do you need to spell out now that you are setting better boundaries in your marriage?

But That Doesn't Sound Submissive

Whenever we talk about a wife setting boundaries, someone asks about the biblical idea of submission (p. 167).

- What is your understanding of submission?

- Read Ephesians 5:21. What does this verse teach about who should be in submission to whom and why?

- What picture of submission do you find in Ephesians 5:24–27?

- Evaluate your marriage (ideally with your spouse) by asking the following questions:
  - Is the husband's relationship with the wife similar to Christ's relationship with the church? How is it similar? How is it different?

  - Does the wife have free choice or is she "under the law" and feeling wrath, guilt, insecurity, and alienation, feelings that the Bible promises the law will bring (Rom. 4:15; Gal. 5:4; James 2:10)?

  - Does the husband offer the wife grace and unconditional love?

- Is the wife in a position of "no condemnation" (Rom. 8:1) or does her husband fail to "wash her" (cf. Eph. 5:26) of all guilt?

We may feel as if we are loving our spouse with grace and unconditional love, but is that what he or she is experiencing? Listen to what your spouse has to say to you (p. 161).

- Read Ephesians 5:28–29. How do these verses undermine the idea of slavelike submission?

Christ never takes away our will or asks us to do something hurtful. He never pushes us past our limits. He never uses us as objects. He gave himself up for us, and he takes care of us as he would his own body (p. 168).

We have never seen a "submission problem" that was not actually a "control problem" at its root.

- Why does this make sense?

- How would you expect a controlling husband to act when his wife starts setting clear boundaries and putting biblical limits on hurtful behavior?

When the partners in a marriage set boundaries, the marriage can then grow and develop (p. 168).

A Question of Balance

Many dimensions need to be balanced in a marriage relationship. Problems come when the balance is not mutual. Remember Meredith and Paul? She was in charge of togetherness, and he was in charge of separateness rather then both of them being responsible for both (p. 169).

- Is there mutual balance in your marriage?

- Is one spouse always powerful and the other powerless?

- Is one spouse always strong and the other weak?

- Like Meredith and Paul, is one spouse always wanting togetherness and the other separateness?

- Does one spouse always want sex while the other is never interested?

When you find yourself in an unequal relationship, you may lack boundaries. Setting boundaries may correct the imbalance. For example, when Paul set boundaries on Meredith's demands, he forced her to become more independent (pp. 169–170).

- What other issues in your marriage seem out of mutual balance? Disciplining the children? Spending money?

- Where do you need to set boundaries? What will be your first step?

It is often easy to see problems and quite difficult to make the hard choices and take the risks that can result in healthy change (p. 170).

Resolution

Let's look at the steps toward personal change in a marital relationship. Work through these nine steps for every boundary conflict that arises in your marriage (pp. 171–173).

- Inventory the Symptom—What is the problem? Do you and your spouse agree to take action to solve it?

- Identify the Specific Boundary Problem—What boundary issue is behind the symptom you identified above? Who is having trouble saying no? Who is having trouble hearing no?

- Find the Origins of the Conflict—What did you experience and therefore learn in your family of origin that you are now transferring to your marriage? What fears, expectations, or self-doubts, for instance, are affecting how you relate to your partner?

- Take in the Good—What support system is offering you the strength you need (Eccl. 4:12) as you learn to set boundaries? Where can you go for help as you develop your boundaries?

- Practice—Who are some safe people with whom you can practice your new boundaries? When will you tell one of them no, share an opinion that is different, or give something without expecting anything in return?

- Say No to the Bad—What bad in your marriage—what abuse, what unreasonable demands—do you need to put limits on? Remember the parable of the talents (Matt. 25:14–30): there is no growth without risk and a facing up to fear.

- Forgive—Unforgiving people allow other people to control them. Who are you allowing to control you because you are not forgiving them?

- Become Proactive—Set some boundaries instead of letting your spouse be in control. What do you want to do? What will you do to reach that goal? What will your limits be in the out-of-control areas of your relationship? What will you no longer allow yourself to be a party to? What will you no longer tolerate? What consequences will you set?

- Learn to Love in Freedom and Responsibility—The goal of boundaries is love coming out of freedom. You can freely choose to "lay down [your] life" for a friend (John 15:13) and serve others as Christ himself served. Where are you still giving out of a sense of guilt and obligation, out of a self-centeredness that hopes to receive in return, or out of boundaryless compliance? To whom can you give something (be specific) simply because you want to? Do so! This kind of practice will help you learn to love freely.

Setting and receiving firm boundaries with your spouse can lead to a much greater intimacy. Take the risk, knowing that the rewards can be very worthwhile (p. 173).

Prayer

Gracious and generous God, I thank you for the gift of marriage, this continuing process of two becoming one in you. As you work in my marriage, teach me to respect the personhood of my spouse so that ours is a godly union—not an unhealthy enmeshment—that glorifies you. Teach me to be honest and to take responsibility for my feelings, desires, attitudes, behaviors, choices, values, and limits, and to be lovingly responsible to my spouse when my confronting him or her results in pain. Help me to communicate my boundaries clearly and unapologetically and to back them up with actions. Help me to take the risks I need to take in my marriage, knowing that you will be with me. I pray in Jesus' name. Amen.

Chapter 8

Boundaries and Your Children

Of all the areas in which boundaries are crucial, none is more relevant than that of raising children. How we approach boundaries and child rearing will have enormous impact on the characters of our kids—how they develop values, how well they do in school, what friends they pick, whom they marry, and how well they do in a career (p. 176).

The Importance of Family

Our Creator God, who is love (1 John 4:8), wants to fill up his universe with beings who care for him and for each other (p. 177).

    God first picked the nation Israel to be his children. After centuries of resistance by Israel, however, God chose the church. The body of Christ, whose role it is to multiply God's love and character, is often described as a family (p. 177).

- What does Paul teach about God's choice in Romans 11:11?

- What God-given role does the body of Christ have on earth? See Matthew 28:19–20; John 17:21; Acts 1:8; and 1 Corinthians 5:11–13.

- What do the following verses say about the family of God?
  - Galatians 6:10

  - Ephesians 2:19

  - 1 Timothy 3:15

The passages you looked at above show how God "thinks family." He explains his heart as a parent would. He's a daddy, and he likes his job (p. 177).

- How and when has the church been a family to you? How has the church been a source of disappointment or pain? How has God loved you through his church?

The Bible's portrayal of our heavenly Father helps show us how parenting is a vital part of bringing God's own character to this planet in our children (p. 177).

Boundaries and Responsibility

God, the good parent, wants to help us—his children—grow up (p. mature in the Lord, we learn how to take responsibility for our live as parents, we are to teach our children about responsibility. Second ing our children learn how to form strong attachments—how to bon them a sense of responsibility, an understanding of what they are re and not responsible for, the ability to say no and to accept no (p. 177

- According to Ephesians 4:13, what is God's goal for us, his children?

- What did you learn about boundaries when you were a child? Did you learn to hate them? Fear them? Respect them? Develop them?

- How do you respond when others set limits on you? Do you have a tantrum or sulk? Do you comply in order to keep the peace?

- What have your own children learned about boundaries up to this point?

- How do your children respond when others set limits on them? Do they have a tantrum or sulk? Do they comply in order to keep the peace?

You may have realized that you, as well as your children, need to work on boundaries—developing your own and respecting other people's. Remember that, for adults, the relearning process is not easy (pp. 177–178)!

Instilling vs. Repairing Boundaries

An older woman watching a young mother struggling to get her youngster to sit on a chair by himself wisely said, "Do it now, dear. Discipline the child now—and you might just survive adolescence." Developing boundaries in young children is that proverbial ounce of prevention. If we teach responsibility, limit setting, and delay of gratification early on, our children's later years will be much smoother (Prov. 22:6) (p. 178).

- Think about your adolescence and, if you can remember, your childhood. Could your adolescence have been predicted by the way you were disciplined or not disciplined as a young child? Explain how what you learned or didn't learn as a child affected your adolescent years.

- Which of these areas, if any—responsibility, limit setting, and delay of gratification—are you still working on for yourself?

- What are you doing to teach your children:
  - Responsibility

  - Limit setting

  - Delay of gratification

Age-appropriate boundary tasks and ideas about teaching children—of any age—responsibility, limit setting, and delay of gratification will come later in the lesson (p. 178).

Boundary Development in Children

When we talk about children and the work of boundary development, we are talking about the work of learning responsibility. As we teach our children the merits and limits of responsibility, we teach them autonomy and prepare them to take on the tasks of adulthood (p. 178).

The Scriptures have much to say about the role of boundary setting in child rearing—about discipline or, according to the original Greek and Hebrew, "teaching." Good child rearing involves preventive training and practice as well as correctional consequences. This follows God's model (p. 178).

- The positive facets of discipline are proactivity, prevention, and instruction (Eph. 6:4). Give specific examples of each of these positive aspects and make them appropriate to the ages and behaviors of your children.

- The negative facets of discipline are correction, chastisement, and consequences (Prov. 15:10). Give specific examples of each of these negative aspects and again make them appropriate to the ages and behaviors of your children.

- Now give an example of how you could use consequences to help set limits for your children. Use a specific situation that you are currently dealing with.

God uses practice—trial and error—to help us grow up. Think about how God has taught you certain things (p. 179).

- What mistakes have you learned from?

- How has God trained you "to distinguish good from evil" (Heb. 5:14)?

- How has practice helped you form boundaries?

- How do you view and respond to the practice your children need to do? Do you allow them to fail and learn new things? Why not?

Discipline is an external boundary designed to develop internal boundaries in our children. It provides a structure of safety until the child has structure enough in his character to not need it (p. 179).

- What internal boundaries are you seeing in your children?

- In what areas are your children currently practicing setting boundaries? How is your discipline helping them?

At this point, let's distinguish between discipline and punishment (pp. 179–180).

- What is your understanding of the difference between discipline and punishment?

Punishment is paying a penalty for breaking the law. It doesn't leave a lot of room for practice (Rom. 6:23; James 2:10), and it's not a great teacher. Punishment doesn't leave much room for mistakes. And punishment focuses on the past (p. 180).

- What did you learn from being punished when you were growing up?

- What are you trying to teach your children through punishment?

In contrast to punishment, discipline is not payment for a wrong. It's the natural law of God: our actions reap consequences. Unlike punishment that looks back, discipline looks forward: the lessons we learn from discipline help us to not make the same mistakes again (Heb. 12:10) (p. 180).

- When, if ever, did your parents effectively use consequences to help you learn? What did those consequences teach you?

- Where could you be using consequences to give your children the chance to practice and learn?

God disciplines us because he loves us, and we are to discipline our children out of love for them. In both cases, the love frees us and our children to make mistakes without fear of judgment and without fear of losing the relationship. This ability to practice in safety will encourage practice and, with consequences and guidance, maturity (p. 180).

- In what areas of life are you currently practicing?

- What does it mean to you and your efforts that God will not judge you or withdraw his love from you?

- As they practice the various skills of life, do your children know that you will not judge them or withdraw your love from them?

As you continue the overwhelming task of parenting, ask God to be with you, giving you wisdom, patience, strength, and love. And keep in mind that he is with you, his child, even as you parent your children (p. 180).

The Boundary Needs of Children

The ability to set limits and establish boundaries—learned when we are children—pays enormous dividends throughout our life (p. 181).

Self-Protection

Human babies are less able to take care of themselves than animal babies. The demanding minute-by-minute task of protection falls to the parents during the newborn months. The parents, however, must gradually pass on the task of protection to their children so that they can protect themselves (Ps. 25:1) (p. 181).

- Review the experiences of Jimmy and Paul (pp. 181–183). Look closely at how they were raised. What pointers can you draw from Jimmy's parents?

- Which of your own behaviors do Paul's parents remind you of? What behaviors could you replace those with?

A hallmark of Jimmy's family was permission to disagree. His parents never withdrew their love or punished him for disagreeing. Instead, they listened to his reasoning and, when appropriate, would change their minds. Jimmy was also given a vote in some family matters. His was a family who took boundary limits seriously enough to give their children the opportunity to practice and develop the skill (pp. 181–183).

Taking Responsibility for One's Needs

The second fruit of developing boundaries is our children's ability to take owner-ship of, or responsibility for, their own needs. God intends for us to know when we're hungry, lonely, in trouble, overwhelmed, or in need of a break—and then to take the initiative to get what we need. Boundaries play a primary role in this process. Our limits create a spiritual and emotional space between ourselves and others that allows us to hear and understand our needs (p. 184).

- The best thing parents can do to help children experience their own individual needs is to encourage the verbal expression of those needs, even when they don't "go with the family flow." When children are free to ask for something—even though they might not receive it—they develop a sense of what they need. What do you think your children feel free to ask for? What needs do they seem free to express?

- Look again at page 185 and the four suggestions about how to help your children develop a sense of what they need. Choose one to start incorporating into your family. What will be your first step and when will you take it? What kind of modeling might you do to encourage your children?

The first aspect of taking ownership of one's needs is to identify them. The second aspect of taking ownership is to initiate responsible caretaking for ourselves—as opposed to placing the burden on someone else. We must allow our children to ex-perience the painful consequences of their own irresponsibility and mistakes. This is the "training" of Hebrews 5:14 and the "discipline" of Hebrews 12 (p. 185).

- As the four convictions listed on page 186 reflect, our children (and we ourselves) need a sense of "my life is up to me." If you haven't had this understanding throughout your life, how could it have helped you? Or, if you have been blessed with this knowledge, how has it helped you through the years?

- In the parable of the talents (Matt. 25:14–30), God calls us to use our talents in productive ways and reminds us that we will be accountable for what we do with our lives. What do you think God's response will be to the excuses that you have made along the way?

We are deeply influenced by our backgrounds and the various stressors of life, but we are ultimately responsible for what we do with our injured, immature souls. Wise parents keep injuries to their children to the absolute minimum by allowing them to undergo only "safe suffering." They allow their children to make age-appropriate decisions and experience age-appropriate consequences (p. 186).

- Remember how Pat's parents helped her learn to budget (page 186)? What age-appropriate responsibilities and consequences can you establish for your children?

It's important to tie consequences as closely to the actions of the child as possible (Heb. 5:8). This best replicates real life. We love our children and want what is best for them. And what is best is not bailing them out but allowing them to experience their failures just as our loving God allows us to experience ours (pp. 186–187).

- What logical and age-appropriate consequences can you allow when it comes to your child's homework assignments?

Having a Sense of Control and Choice

Children need to have a sense of control and choice in their life. They need to see themselves not as the dependent, helpless pawns of parents, but as choosing, willing, initiative-taking agents of their own lives. If children aren't allowed to make decisions and skin their knees as a result, they become atrophied in their change-making abilities, an important part of the image of God that they are to reflect. Children need a sense that their lives are largely theirs to determine, within the province of God's sovereignty (Matt. 6:33). Being free to make decisions teaches them to appreciate the consequences of the choices they make (p. 188).

- What do you like about the way Sal dealt with Pamela's objection to going to the dentist? What, if anything, didn't you like?

- Where can you apply Sal's approach with your children? Be specific in your plans—and then take action.

- Godly parenting seeks to help children learn to think, make decisions, and master their environment in all aspects of life. What are you doing to achieve this important parenting goal?

- What did your parents do to teach you to make good decisions? What can you learn from them?

- What happens when parents make their children's choices for them and try to prevent them from making painful decisions?

Delaying Gratification of Goals

The word now *was made for young children. It's where they live. Yet at some point in our development we learn the value of "later," of delaying one good for a greater good. We learn to say no to our impulses, wishes, and desires for some gain down the road—and Jesus is our prime example (Heb. 12:2). Learning how to delay gratification helps our children become self-sufficient adults instead of sluggards who are always in crisis. It also helps them learn to have a goal and work towards it (p. 189).*

- What benefits do you see in teaching delay of gratification to your children?

- How did you learn—or how are you learning—the value of delaying gratification (Luke 14:28)?

- How can you begin or continue to teach your children the value of delaying gratification?

Respecting the Limits of Others

From an early age, children need to be able to accept the limits of parents, siblings, and friends. They need to realize that the world doesn't revolve around them. Accepting limits teaches us to take responsibility for ourselves. The longer we hate and resist the limits of others, the more dependent on them we will be (Prov. 19:27). We will come to expect others to take care of us, rather than simply taking care of ourselves (p. 190).

- What are the lifelong benefits of learning this truth? What are some of the consequences of not learning this truth?

- The list on page 190 identifies various sources of no in life. At which of the eight stages did you learn to accept the boundary of other people's no? Why is it better to learn to accept no from the sources early in the list instead of later in the list?

If we don't teach our children to take a no, someone who loves them far less may take on the job. Most parents would much rather spare their children from such suffering. The earlier we teach limits, the better (p. 191).

- Another reason why accepting the limits of others is important for kids is that heeding others' boundaries helps children love. Explain the connection between the Golden Rule (treating others as you want to be treated), respecting limits, and learning to love (Matt. 7:12).

- How did you learn that you can hurt people you love and that your actions matter? What are you doing to teach your children this lesson?

We need to help our children realize that their actions impact other people. When they are aware of other people's needs and hurts, they learn to be responsible for what they do and say. This lesson can keep our children from being self-centered or controlling. Then they can become loving people (p. 191).

Seasonal Boundaries: Age-Appropriate Limit Training

We parents need to consider our children's developmental needs and abilities if we are to avoid asking them to do too much or too little toward learning limits and developing boundaries. This section provides an outline of the age-appropriate boundary tasks for your children (pp. 192–199).

Birth to Five Months

- What are the tasks a newborn needs to accomplish?

- What can parents do to help their newborn accomplish these tasks?

- What are you doing to help your newborn?

A newborn needs to develop a sense of belonging and of being safe and welcome. Providing security for the infant is more important than setting limits or teaching delay of gratification (a process that should begin only gradually during the first year and should begin in full force after the first year of life) (pp. 192–194).

Five to Ten Months

- Explain why the last half of the first year of life is called the "hatching" phase. What is a child learning?

- What can parents do to help their five- to ten-month-old child meet his or her needs for attachment as well as separation?

- What are you doing to help your child?

To encourage attempts at separateness, parents need to allow their child to be fascinated with people and objects. Make the home a safe place for the baby to explore. At the same time, tend to the child's needs for bonding and emotional safety (p. 194).

Ten to Eighteen Months

- What are babies doing during this "practicing" stage of their young life?

- What is a healthy response to your child's no?

- What can you do to start teaching limits and consequences to your little one?

Saying no is your child's way of finding out whether taking responsibility for her life has good results—or whether it causes someone to withdraw. So, as parents, learn to rejoice in your baby's no. At the same time, help your child see that she is not the center of the universe and that there are consequences for her actions. Teach her those consequences without quenching her sense of excitement and her interest in the world (pp. 194–195).

Eighteen to Thirty-six Months

- What are the goals and the primary tasks of this stage?

- What role will a wise parent assume with a child who wants her no respected but who is not always willing to respect the parent's no?

- Comment on the four-step process of discipline outlined on page 188. Why do you think it would be effective? What, if any, drawbacks do you see in it? When will you try this approach, if you're not using it already?

Respect your child's no whenever appropriate, yet maintain your own firm no. Pick your battles carefully. Enjoy the fun times, but consistently and uniformly keep solid limits with your child. At this age, children can learn the rules of the house as well as the consequences for breaking them (pp. 195–196).

Three to Five Years

- What crucial work is your child doing during this developmental stage?

- What can parents do to help their three- to five-year-old child deal with their budding sexuality?

- What are you doing to help your child? How are you allowing your same-sex child to identify and compete? How are you dealing with the possessiveness of your opposite-sex child?

Children identify with—and at the same time compete with—the same-sex parent, and wish to marry the opposite-sex parent. Mature parents keep the lines between parent and child clear (pp. 196–197).

Six to Eleven Years

- What work is a child doing during this latency period, also known as years of industry?

- What boundary tasks are parents working on for themselves in order to encourage healthy boundaries in their children?

- What issues are most challenging for you as a parent right now?

Parents play a crucial role during this stage as their children are doing boundary work such as learning delay of gratification, goal orientation, and time budgeting. Parents need to let consequences teach without being the rescuer (p. 197).

Eleven to Eighteen Years

- What issues make this final step before adulthood frightening yet exciting for both child and parents?

- What shift has probably begun to take place in your parenting? What are you doing differently now?

- What issues are most challenging for you as a parent right now?

Wise parents struggle with the question, "How can I help my children survive on their own?" Again, allowing their children to deal with consequences of their behavior can teach them much about boundaries and life (pp. 197–199).

Types of Discipline

- Where have you turned for input about disciplining your child?

- What effective methods have you incorporated into your family?

- What child-rearing issues (spanking, time-outs, restrictions, allowances, etc.) do you have questions about? What are those questions?

- Review the four points on consequences and boundaries listed on pages 199–200. What do these points say to the questions you identified above?

We parents have the challenging task and sober responsibility of teaching our children to have an internal sense of boundaries and to respect the boundaries of others. There are no guarantees that our training will be heeded. Yet as we learn about our own boundary issues, take responsibility for them, and grow up ourselves, we increase our kids' chances to learn boundaries for the adult world where they'll need them every day (Eph. 4:13) (p. 200).

Prayer

Father God, I thank you for the model you give me as I try to answer the high calling of parenting. Teach me the following so that, in turn, I can teach my children to protect themselves by saying no: to express needs so that they can learn to take responsibility for getting them met, to give my children a sense of control in life by giving them appropriate choices, to delay gratification, and to respect the limits of others and learn to take care of themselves so that they can learn to love. Give me the wisdom I need to teach responsibility through the use of consequences and the wisdom to know when to let go and stand back. Give me the courage to let my children experience their failures, and patience and strength each step of the way. May my children know unconditional love as they practice this business called "life" — an unconditional love that will point them to you. And, God, I know that my children are your children first. May I entrust them, ultimately, to your care. I pray in your Son's name. Amen.

Chapter 9

Boundaries and Work

Work is essentially good. It existed before the Fall. It was always part of God's plan for humanity to subdue and rule the earth (Gen. 1:28). As a result of the Fall, those tasks became more difficult (Gen. 3:17–19), the tendency toward disowner-ship arose (Gen. 3:11–13), and work and love became separated from one another ("want to" became "should," increasing our wish to rebel, sparking our anger, and arousing our motivations to do the wrong thing [Rom. 5:20, 4:15, 7:5]). Let's consider now how boundaries can help resolve many work-related problems and help you be happier and more fulfilled in the work you do (pp. 201–202).

Work and Character Development

Christians often have a warped perspective on work. Unless someone is working "in the ministry," they may see work as secular (p. 202).

Think about your own work for a moment (and being a full-time, at-home parent definitely counts as work).

- What work do you do?

- What is your perspective on your work? Do you consider it a ministry?

- How does your perspective affect your attitude toward your work?

Now consider what the Bible teaches.

- What does Paul command believers in Colossians 3:23?

- How could doing your work as "for the Lord" impact, if not revolutionize, your work?

All of us—not only full-time ministers—have gifts and talents we are to use to serve God and his people (p. 202).

- What is the significance of the fact that, through his parables, Jesus addresses money, completing tasks, faithful stewardship of a job, and honest emotional dealings in work?

In his parables, Jesus teaches a work ethic based on love under God. In our work, we reflect the image of God, who is himself a worker, a manager, a creator, a developer, a steward, and a healer. To be a Christian is to be a colaborer with God in the human community. Furthermore, work is the place we develop our character in preparation for the work we will do forever. With that in mind, let's look at how setting boundaries in our work can help us grow spiritually (pp. 202–203).

- Consider your work. What aspects of your work reflect the image of God as a worker?

- How is God using your work to make you more Christlike?

Problems in the Workplace

A lack of boundaries creates problems in the workplace. Let's see how applying boundaries can solve some of these.

Problem #1: Getting Saddled with Another Person's Responsibilities

- Are you, like Susie (pp. 203–204), being saddled with another person's responsibilities? List those tasks.

- When are you going to confront the "Jack" in your life? And what will you say to him or her?

- How will you respond to that person's anger?

- What will you do when that person wants an explanation?

- What rule of thumb can help you determine whether helping out a colleague is enabling that person or doing a favor and sacrificing?

Favors and sacrifices done out of love are part of the Christian life, and that is what you are doing if your giving is helping the other person become better. The Bible requires responsible action out of the one who is given to. If you do not see it after a season, set limits (Luke 13:9) (p. 205).

Problem #2: Working Too Much Overtime

• How much overtime do you tend to work? Be honest!

• If the amount of overtime is excessive, why do you continue to log so many hours? What is keeping you from talking to your supervisor and setting limits?

• Review the steps suggested on pages 206–207. When will you start implementing these?

• Even after you have confronted your boss, he or she may continue to make unreasonable demands on you. What options do you have if you realize you need to look elsewhere for a job?

Your job overload is your responsibility and your problem. You need to own the problem and do something about it. Stop being a victim of an impossible situation and start setting limits (Matt. 10:14) (p. 207).

Problem #3: Misplaced Priorities

• Effective workers strive to do excellent work, and they spend their time on the most important things. Are your standards as high as they should be? Where should they be higher? Where should your standards be lower? What less important tasks could you spend less time and effort on? What are your three most important tasks or responsibilities?

- Having limits will force you to prioritize and to work smart. (We all know how work grows to fill the time you set aside for it!) Establish a time budget for yourself. List the various aspects of your work and assign the maximum amount of time you will spend with each. Then start living by this schedule (but don't expect perfection right away).

Moses' father-in-law Jethro saw that Moses was going to wear himself out. Moses had allowed good work to go too far (Exod. 18:14–27). Limits on good things keep them good (p. 209).

Problem #4: Difficult Coworkers

- The Law of Power says that you only have the power to change yourself. You can't change another person. What does this law say to you about difficult coworkers?

- How are you currently relating to a difficult coworker? What are your reactions and responses to him or her? Make your answer as specific as possible.

- Look carefully at the preceding answer. What can you do to change yourself and your contact, interactions, and reactions to that person?

Focusing on the other person gives him or her power over you. You must refuse to allow that person to affect you. The real problem lies in how you are relating to a difficult coworker. You must change your reactions to that person (Matt. 18:15–18) (p. 209).

Problem #5: Critical Attitudes

- How are you dealing with the critic in your workplace? Are you trying to win him or her over? Do you let him or her make you angry? Are you internalizing the criticism and getting down on yourself? How effective is your way of handling the criticism?

- You can't change a critic. Allow those people to be who they are, but keep yourself separate from them and do not internalize their opinion of you. What can you do to separate from them? What truths can you remind yourself of when you find yourself beginning to internalize a critic's words?

- Review the suggestions on page 210. What avenue will you choose to follow in dealing with your critic?

Avoid trying to gain the approval of a critic and avoid getting in arguments and discussions (Prov. 9:7–8). Stay separate. Keep your boundaries. Don't get sucked into their game (p. 210).

Problem #6: Conflicts with Authority

- If you are having trouble with your boss, the issue may be transference. Transference is experiencing feelings in the present that really belong to some unfinished business in the past, and authority figures in the workplace may trigger such a reaction. Who in your workplace do you have strong reactions to? With whom do you feel especially competitive?

- Whom does that person remind you of? Does their behavior remind you of the way your parents or other family member treated you? How is that person's personality like your mother or father's? Or, if the issue is one of competition, what competitive relationship from the past are you being reminded of?

- What old patterns are you acting out as a result of the similarities you've just identified?

- What will you do to face these feelings so that you can begin to see people as they really are and not through your own distortions? Be specific about your plan—and implement it right away!

Whenever you experience strong feelings, see them as your responsibility. This will lead you to any unfinished business and healing, as well as keep you from acting irrationally toward co-workers and bosses (Gal. 1:10) (p. 211).

Problem #7: Expecting Too Much of Work

- What unrealistic expectations do you have for your work? What unmet childhood needs do you hope to have met there?

- What does this perspective help you see about your struggles in the workplace? What do you now understand about those workplace dynamics that have been difficult for you?

- Where else can you turn—or are you turning—for nurturing, relationship, self-esteem, and approval?

Make sure you are meeting your needs for support and emotional repair outside of work. Get your relationship needs met outside of work as well. Then, when you go to work, keep your boundaries firm. Protect your hurt places when you are in the workplace, which is not set up to heal and may also wound unintentionally (p. 212).

Problem #8: Taking Work-Related Stress Home

- What emotions from the workplace do you tend to bring home?

- What relationship is the catalyst for most of those emotions? Why are the successes and failures of work so able to bring you up or down? How will you go about determining answers to these questions?

- Evaluate the time, energy, and other resources you are putting into your job. What is your job costing you in terms of your personal life, your relationships, your health?

- What limits will you set on your job? (Review Problem #2: Working Too Much Overtime, pages 205–207 of the text.)

Find out your own limits and live by them. Set good boundaries for your work so that you can enjoy a healthy emotional life and a life that is in balance (Micah 6:8) (pp. 212–213).

Problem #9: Disliking Your Job

- Many people dislike their job because they have never been able to find a true work identity. Is your dislike of your job chronic? Could it be because you are in a job that you never really wanted for yourself? If so, whose expectations influenced you? What pressures, perhaps from friends or the culture, guided you instead of your own gifts, talents, wants, desires, and dreams?

- While you may not have had strong boundaries when you began the job you currently have, your boundaries may be stronger now. So what will you do, in partnership with God, to find out who you really are and what kind of work you are made for? Be specific about your strategy. You might begin by asking people who know you well what kind of work they could see you doing.

- Take time to consider dreams, loves, talents, and desires. What do these aspects of you suggest about the work you would enjoying doing?

As you consider job possibilities, have a realistic expectation of yourself based on who you really are, your own true self with your own particular gifts. This time, stand up against others' expectations of you (Rom. 12:2) (pp. 213–214).

Finding Your Life's Work

Finding your life's work involves taking risks. You need to firmly establish your identity, separating yourself from those you are attached to and following your desires. You must take ownership of how you feel, how you think, and what you want. You must assess your talents and limitations. And then you must begin to step out as God leads you (p. 214).

- Consider where you are in your search for your life's work. What is the next risk, in the series outlined above, that you need to take?

- What specific actions does that particular risk call you to make? And when will you take action?

- What promise do you find in Psalm 37:4–5?

- What warning do you find in Ecclesiastes 11:9?

God wants you to discover and use your gifts to his glory. He will also hold you accountable for what you do. Look at your work as a partnership between you and God. He has given you gifts, and he wants you to develop them. Commit your way to the Lord, and you will find your work identity and, with it, satisfaction (p. 214).

Prayer

Almighty God, thank you for the work you've called me to do. May I see it as a ministry and work to bring honor to you. Give me wisdom and courage to deal with the specific problems I face in the workplace, and to set the boundaries I need to set in regards to my work. When those problems are the result of unmet childhood needs or unfinished business from the past, I ask you to bring healing. Finally, as I work for you, help me to clearly see what is important and to always strive to do excellent work. I pray in Jesus' name. Amen.

Chapter 10

Boundaries and Your Self

In this lesson, instead of looking outward at our interaction with other people, we'll look at our responsibility to control our own bodies (1 Thess. 4:4) and at our own internal boundary conflicts. This can get a little touchy (pp. 215–216).

Our Out-of-Control Soul

As you work through this lesson, we encourage you to look humbly at yourself, to ask for feedback from others, to listen to people you trust, and to confess, "I was wrong." Doing so paves the way for healing and wholeness (p. 216).

Eating

- Do you use food as a false boundary, to avoid intimacy by gaining weight and becoming less attractive?

- Do you binge, finding the comfort of food less scary than the prospect of real relationships (1 John 4:18)?

Money

- Which of the following areas do you struggle with?
  - Impulse spending
  - Careless budgeting
  - Living beyond your means
  - Credit problems
  - Chronically borrowing from friends
  - Ineffectual savings plans
  - Working more to pay all the bills
  - Enabling others

- How could your love of money be the root of evil in your life (1 Tim. 6:10)? In what circumstances do you especially feel like a servant of money (Prov. 22:7)?

Time

- How do you deal with deadlines? Are you a "do-ahead" person or a "last-minute" person? How well do you manage your time? Do you consider yourself able to get a lot done or are you unable to get everything done that needs to be done? Are you able to get places on time? When you wake up in the morning, do you already feel behind?

- If you feel that your time is out of control, which one (or more) of the following causes may be behind it (Eph. 5:16)?
  - A false sense of omnipotence ("No problem! I'll do it!")
  - Being overly responsible for the feelings of others
  - Lack of realistic anxiety
  - Living too much in the present to plan ahead
  - Rationalization ("They're my friends. They'll understand.")

Task Completion

- Are you a good starter but a poor finisher? Have you started an exercise program, a diet, a Bible study program, or a Scripture memorization plan several times without getting very far? Do your creative ideas somehow never pan out?

- If you're a poor finisher, which one of the following causes may be behind that tendency (Prov. 21:5)?
  - Resistance to structure
  - Fear of success and the envy, criticism, and loss of friends which may follow
  - Lack of follow-through
  - Distractibility
  - The inability to delay gratification
  - The inability to say no to other pressures, people, and projects

The Tongue

- Are you pleased with how often you use your tongue to bless, empathize, identify, encourage, confront and exhort others?

- Rather than following the biblical injunctions for restraint (Prov. 10:19, 17:27; Matt. 12:36), do you use your tongue too frequently for some of the following? Which ones?
  - Talking nonstop to hide from intimacy
  - Dominating conversations to control others
  - Gossiping
  - Making sarcastic remarks, expressing indirect hostility
  - Threatening someone, expressing direct hostility
  - Flattering, instead of authentically praising
  - Seducing

Sexuality

- Are you caught up in any out-of-control sexual behavior (compulsive masturbation, compulsive heterosexual or homosexual relationships, pornography, prostitution, exhibitionism, voyeurism, obscene phone calls, indecent liberties, child molestation, incest, rape)?

- God calls us to live in the light (Eph. 5:8–11). What will you do to bring the behavior you just confessed out of the dark, allowing it to be healed before it becomes more of a tyrant?

Alcohol and Substance Abuse

- Are you abusing alcohol and/or drugs (1 Cor. 3:16–17)? Are you being honest with yourself as you evaluate your use?

- Are you dealing with divorce, job loss, financial havoc, or medical problems because of your use of alcohol and/or drugs?

- Having surveyed seven areas where an out-of-control soul manifests itself, what have you learned about the condition of your internal boundaries? Where are they strong? Where would you like them to be stronger?

Why Doesn't My "No" Work?

As you read about the out-of-control areas above, you may have felt defeated and frustrated with yourself. You probably could identify with one or more of the problem areas, and you probably are no stranger to the discouragement of not having mature boundaries in these internal areas. Why doesn't our no work on ourselves? Consider the following three reasons (p. 222).

We are our own worst enemies. It is easier to set limits on other people than it is to set limits on ourselves (p. 222).

• Where do you find yourself not doing what you want to do and doing what you don't want to do? Paul struggled with this problem (Rom. 7:15–19). What internal problems do you struggle with?

• How forgiving are you of yourself when you fall? How honest with yourself are you? Asked from another angle, what does the critical person in your head tell you when you struggle?

Since the Fall, our human instinct has been to withdraw from relationship when we're in trouble, when we most need other people (Gen. 3:10). Whether our boundary issue is food, substances, sex, time, projects, the tongue, or money, we can't solve it in a vacuum. The more we isolate ourselves, the harder the struggle becomes (pp. 223–224).

• Is it your pattern to withdraw from relationship when you're in trouble? As a result, are you choosing not to tell anyone about the struggle you mentioned above? Are trying to deal with it on your own?

- What do the images of the vine (John 15:1–6) and the body (Eph. 4:16) and the instruction of James 5:16 teach about the importance of being connected to God and his people as you confront your self-boundary problems?

We try to use willpower to solve our boundary problems. We make a vow to God and ourselves that we will stop a certain behavior. If all we need is our will to overcome evil, we certainly don't need a Savior (1 Cor. 1:17). Will is strengthened by relationship (Deut. 3:28)—the power of the relationship promised in the Cross (pp. 224–225).

- How well have you succeeded with your vows to change?

- Explain how this approach makes an idol out of the will. Colossians 2:20–23 may help.

Establishing Boundaries with Yourself

Learning to mature in self-boundaries is not easy. Remember that God desires your maturity and self-control even more than you do (1 Thess. 2:11–12). A modified version of the boundary checklist we saw in Lesson 6 can help you begin to develop limits on your out-of-control behavior (p. 226).

What are the symptoms?

Let the symptoms be a road map as you begin to identify the particular boundary problem you're having (Matt. 16:1–3) (p. 226).

- What destructive fruit (depression, anxiety, panic, phobias, rage, relationship struggles, isolation, work problems, psychosomatic problems, compulsive behaviors) are you experiencing because you are not able to say no to yourself?

What are the roots?

Pinpointing the causes of your self-boundary problems will help you understand your own contribution to the problem (how you have sinned), your developmental injuries (how you have been sinned against), and the significant relationships that may have contributed to the problem (Matt. 7:17) (pp. 226–227).

- Which of the following may be roots of your self-boundary conflicts?
  - Lack of training in setting limits, in facing consequences for your actions, or in delaying gratification
  - Rewarded destructiveness: learning that out-of-control behavior brings relationships
  - A distortion of legitimate, God-given needs
  - Fear of relationships—your out-of-control behavior keeps people away
  - A deep hunger for love that was not met in the first few years of your life
  - Being raised in a legalistic environment—now you're rebelling
  - Covering emotional hurt that came when you were neglected or abused as a child

What is the boundary conflict?

- Do you have weak or nonexistent boundaries in relation to eating, money, time, task completion, the tongue, sexuality, or alcohol and substance abuse? Ask God for insight into what other areas of your life are out of control.

Who needs to take ownership?

- Your behavior pattern may be directly traceable to family problems, neglect, abuse, or trauma. Even so, explain what it means that you are responsible for your boundary conflicts (Gal. 6:5).

What do you need?

- You are severely hampered in gaining either insight into or control over yourself when you are disconnected from God's people. Safe, trusting, grace-and-truth relationships are spiritual and emotional fuel. What relationships are giving you this fuel? Or where can you go to begin establishing such relationships (Matt. 5:1–6)?

- Read Luke 11:24–26. What does Jesus say in this parable about the problem of symptomatic relief? What risk are you taking when you don't fill your "house" with the love of God and others?

How do you begin?

- Having identified your boundary problem and being willing to take responsibility for it, now you need to *address your real need*. Only then can you deal with the out-of-control behavior. What is the real problem, not the symptomatic problem, you want to deal with?

- As you address your real need, remember that the self-boundary problem will recur, so *allow yourself to fail* (Heb. 5:14). What are some reasons why it is important to embrace failure?

- As you fail to set boundaries on yourself, you need others who will let you know about it in a caring way—and you need to *listen to their empathic feedback*. Who in your life offers empathic feedback that you will listen to? Who speaks truth in love to you?

- When our own lack of love or responsibility causes our suffering, we need to *welcome these consequences as a teacher*. When have consequences taught you lessons that God's teaching and the words of his people have not? What consequences have you or could you experience due to your lack of boundaries and the resulting out-of-control behavior?

- As you hear feedback and suffer consequences, it's important that you *surround yourself with people who are loving and supportive*, but who will not rescue you. Why is an empathic friend more helpful and loving than a critical and parental one (Gal. 6:1)? Than one who rescues you? What kind of friend are you to people with self-boundary problems? Who in your life plays the role of critical, parental friend? Of a rescuer? Of empathic friend?

The five-point formula for developing self-boundaries, which you've just looked at, is cyclical. Every time you go through the cycle—as you deal with real needs, fail, get empathic feedback, suffer consequences, and are restored—you build stronger internal boundaries (pp. 228–232).

If You Are a Victim

Establishing boundaries for yourself is always hard, but it is especially difficult if your boundaries were severely violated in childhood (Ps. 129:1–3) (p. 232).

- What kind of victimization, if any, did you experience (or do you suspect you may have experienced) as a child—verbal, emotional, physical, sexual, other?

- Look again at page 233 and a list of some results of victimization. Which of these have you experienced?

- Our ability to trust ourselves is based on our experience of others as trustworthy. What evidence in your life can you point to that suggests you have trouble trusting others? Trusting yourself (1 John 4:18)?

- Victims often feel that they are public property—that their resources, bodies, and time should be available to others just for the asking. Do you see yourself in this statement? How do you think this contributes to your self-boundary problems (1 Cor. 16:13)?

- Victimization also results in a deep, pervasive sense of being "all-bad," wrong, dirty, or shameful—no matter how affirming others are of their lovableness. Again, do you see yourself in this description? If so, what evidence is there in your life of your inability or failure to take care of yourself because you don't feel that you're worth it (Eph. 1:4–6)?

Boundaries as an Aid to the Victim

Boundary work can help move victims toward restoration and healing, but in many cases such work is most effectively done with professional help. If you are a victim of abuse, we strongly urge you to seek out a counselor who can guide you in establishing and maintaining appropriate boundaries. God can, and does, use such relationships to work great healing in people's lives (p. 234).

- If you are working with a professional, how has he or she helped you do what you couldn't do alone? Are you in counseling that reinforces blame or that helps you take responsibility for your life?

- If you are not yet working with a professional, what is holding you back? Certain ideas about people who get professional help? Questions about how to find someone you can work with? Finances? Fear? Theology?

Prayer

Holy God, I confess to you my out-of-control soul as it manifests itself in my eating/spending/poor use of time/failure to complete tasks/inability to control my tongue/sexuality/alcohol and substance abuse. Thank you that I don't need to rely on my own will to overcome this problem and that instead I can turn to my Savior. Open my eyes, Jesus, to the symptoms of my out-of-control soul, their roots, and my weak or nonexistent boundaries. Show me what needs I'm trying to meet with my out-of-control behavior—and show me better ways to have those needs met. Help me to be responsible for myself. Please provide me with empathic friends, loving and supportive people who can help me. Give me the ability to learn from the consequences of my behaviors, the ability to receive love from friends, and hope in your healing and redeeming power. I pray in Jesus' name. Amen.

Chapter 11

Boundaries and God

More than a book that contains rules, principles, and stories that explain what it is like to exist on this earth, the Bible is a living book about relationship — relationship of God to people, people to God, and people to each other. It is about God as creator, ruler, and redeemer. It communicates the message "Love God and love your neighbor as yourself" (Matt. 22:37–40) — a simple command, but not an easy one to obey. Boundary problems are one reason why obeying God's command to love him and love one another is difficult. The Bible clarifies these boundaries so that we can begin to see who should do what in this labor of love (pp. 235–236).

Respecting Boundaries

We have personal boundaries in our relationship with God. He respects those boundaries, and we need to respect his (p. 236).

First, God respects our boundaries by leaving work for us that only we can do. He also allows us to experience the painful consequences of our behavior so that we will change and not perish (Ezek. 18:23; 2 Peter 3:9) (p. 236).

- What work has God given human beings to do that only we can do? See, for instance, Matthew 25:13–29 and Philippians 2:12.

- What consequences for your behavior has God allowed you to experience so that you would change?

Second, God respects our no. He gives us a choice. When we say no, he allows it and keeps on loving us (p. 236).

- What do the following passages teach about how God responds when we say no to him?

  - Matthew 19:16–22

  - Luke 15:11–24

Remember the story of Jerry and his extramarital affairs (p. 237)?

- What step of honesty did Jerry take that finally made change possible?

- What is God saying to you through Jerry's story? Where do you need to start being brutally honest with yourself about yourself? In what areas of your life are you saying no to God?

- What hope does Jerry's experience give you for what can happen when we are honest about where we are saying no to God?

An honest no will lead us to discover how destructive it is to avoid God and to a real hunger and thirst for righteousness. Until we take responsibility for our boundaries with God—until we can be honest with him and ourselves about where we are saying no to him—we can't ever change our boundaries or allow him to work with them (Matt. 21:28–32) (p. 237).

In our deeper honesty and ownership of our true person, there is room for expressing anger at God (Job 13:3). God wants us to be honest with him. When we own what is within our boundaries, when we bring it into the light, God can transform it with his love. Rest assured that God desires truth in your "inner parts" (Ps. 51:6). He is seeking people who will have a real relationship with him (John 4:23–24) (p. 238).

• Are you comfortable expressing anger at God? Why or why not?

• If you are able to express anger at God, how do you do that?

• If you aren't comfortable being angry at God, what do you fear? Abandonment? Retaliation? Something else?

• What would you like to be angry with God about? Take that step toward a more real relationship with him.

Respecting His Boundaries

God respects our boundaries, and he expects us to respect his. When he makes choices or says no to us, that is God's right, his freedom. If we are to have a real relationship with him, we need to respect that freedom (p. 238).

- When has God said no to you?

- How did you respond to God's no?

- What does this perspective on God's boundaries say to you about that situation?

We call people "bad" because they do not do what we want them to do. We judge them for being themselves, for fulfilling their wishes. We withdraw love from them when they do what they feel is best for them, not what we want them to do (p. 238).

- When have you treated God like this? Be specific.

- What evidence of God's pure love for you do you have even when he does things you don't like? See Romans 5:8 and Hebrews 12:11.

God is free from us, and his freedom allows him to love. Many Bible characters ran into God's freedom and learned to embrace it. As a result, they experienced a deeper relationship with him (p. 239).

- Turn to page 239. What does each of the following men teach you about letting God be God?

  - Job

- Paul (2 Cor. 12:7–10)

- Jesus (Heb. 5:7–10)

- Where do you need to let God be God—free to make choices, free to say no—in your life today?

In the same way that we want others to respect our no, God wants us to respect his. He doesn't want us to make him the bad guy when he makes a choice. We do not like others trying to manipulate or control us with guilt, and neither does he (p. 239).

"I Respectfully Disagree"

Then again, God does not want us to be passive in our relationship with him either. Sometimes, through dialogue with us, he changes his mind. One of the most astounding teachings of the Bible is that we can influence God (Isa. 1:18). It wouldn't be a real relationship if we couldn't (pp. 239–240).

- Read Genesis 18:16–33. What decision did Abraham want God to change?

- How did Abraham approach God? Describe his strategy and suggest why you think it was effective.

- What do these two passages teach about our ability to influence God?
  - Luke 11:5–9

  - Luke 18:1–8

God wants us to respect his boundaries. He doesn't want us to withdraw our love when he says no, but he has nothing at all against our trying to persuade him to change his mind. In fact, he asks us to be tenacious (p. 240).

- Where may God be calling you, through this teaching, to be tenacious and to try to persuade him to change his mind?

However God responds to our requests, we are to respect his wishes and stay in relationship with him (p. 240).

Respecting His Own

In addition to our respecting God's boundaries and his respecting ours, he is a good model for how we should respect our own property. Whenever God decides that "enough is enough," he respects his own property enough to do something to make it better. He takes responsibility for the pain he is feeling and moves to make his life different. He, for instance, lets go of rejecting people and reaches out to some new friends. When we are hurting, we need to take responsibility for our heart and move to make things better, just as God does (pp. 240–241).

God is the ultimate responsibility taker. Read the parable of the wedding banquet in Matthew 22:1–14.

- Summarize the story.

- What responsibility does the king take for the situation at hand? What does he do?

- What does this parable teach about God respecting his own boundaries, and how we should respect our own property?

- Where do you need to be taking responsibility for your pain?

- What do you need to let go of? What do you need to reach out for?

A Real Relationship

Relationship is what the gospel is all about. It is a gospel of "reconciliation" (Rom. 5:11; Col. 1:19–20). It brings hostile parties together (Col. 1:21) and heals relationships between God and humanity and between people (p. 241.

- When have you experienced the reconciling power of the gospel in your life? Be specific about what happened.

- In what relationships do you need to invite the gospel of reconciliation to do its work?

Boundaries are inherent in any relationship God has created, for they define the two parties who are loving each other (p. 242).

- Boundaries between us and God are important to the oneness or unity we have with him (John 17:20–23). Why is knowing the distinct identity of God and of yourself important to a real relationship with him?

- When has being unclear about who God is, and/or who you are as his creation, interfered with your relationship with him? Be specific. Where, if at all, is such lack of clarity interfering now? What are you going to do to clarify your understanding of his boundaries and of your own?

Boundaries help us to be the best we can be—in God's image. They let us see God as he really is. They enable us to negotiate life, fulfilling our responsibilities. If we are trying to do his work for him, we will fail. If we are wishing for him to do our work for us, he will refuse. But if we do our work and God does his, we will find strength in a real relationship with our Creator (p. 242).

Prayer

Loving and forgiving God, you call me to love you and to love people, and I confess to you that I so often fail. I thank you for giving me insight into why, and hope for the development of boundaries so that I will be able to love. Thank you, too, for respecting my boundaries, for giving me work to do, for giving me choices, for allowing me to experience and learn from the consequences of my actions, and for respecting my no. Help me to see clearly when I am saying no to you so that I can come to hunger and thirst for you and your righteousness, and enter into a more real relationship with you. Help me also to be honest about anger I might feel toward you.

You honor my boundaries. Forgive me for not honoring yours. Teach me to respect your right to say no, to trust in your pure love for me, as evidenced in the Cross, and to let you be God. At the same time that I am to let you be God, I thank you for the invitation to not be passive in my relationship with you, for the invitation to be persistent in prayer and tenacious in my requests. Teach me to take responsibility for situations in my life and for the pain I'm feeling. Give me courage when that means letting go of the familiar and reaching out to something new. I look forward to a deeper and more real relationship with you, Almighty God and Gracious Father. Amen.

Part Three

Developing Healthy Boundaries

Chapter 12

Resistance to Boundaries

We have talked about the necessity of boundaries and their immeasurable value in our lives. In fact, we have all but said that life without boundaries is no life at all. But establishing and maintaining boundaries takes a lot of work, discipline, and, most of all, desire (p. 245).

The Driving Force

The driving force behind boundaries has to be desire. We usually know the right thing to do (Matt. 22:37–40), but we are rarely motivated to do it unless there's a good reason. That we should be obedient to God, who tells us to set and maintain boundaries, is certainly the best reason—but it's not always enough. We need to see that what is right is also good for us (Deut. 11:18–21) (p. 245).

- When has seeing that what is right is also good for you helped you do the right thing? Be specific.

- Where are you when it comes to boundaries? Do you understand that setting and maintaining boundaries is right? An act of obedience to God? Good for you?

- Often our pain helps us see that something is good for us. How has your pain contributed to your realization that boundaries are good for you?

Even with the desire for the better life which results from boundaries, we can be reluctant to do the work of boundaries for another reason: it will mean war. There will be skirmishes, battles, disputes, and losses (p. 245).

- Why should we expect to have to fight for our growth? See Ephesians 6:10–13.

God has secured our salvation and our sanctification. In position and principle he has healed us. But we have to work out his image in us (Rom. 8:29; Phil. 2:12) (p. 246).

- What specific things do you think you have to do to work out God's image in you?

Part of the healing process is regaining our boundaries. God has defined who we are and what our limits are so that he can bless us (Ps. 16:5–6), but we are the ones who have to do battle. And the battles fall into two categories: outside resistance and inside resistance (p. 246).

Outside Resistance

Outside resistance is the resistance we get from others as we try to establish and maintain healthy boundaries (pp. 246–247).

Julie had a difficult time with boundaries most of her life. The child of a domineering father and a mother who controlled her with guilt, Julie had been afraid to set boundaries with some people because of their anger and with others because of the guilt she would feel for "hurting them" (pp. 246–247).

- How are you like Julie? Are you afraid of people's anger? Of hurting people? Both?

- Julie learned that people were going to fight hard against her limits. Whom do you expect to fight hard against your limits?

Outside resistance — people fighting against your boundaries — comes in a variety of forms. We're going to look at eight of them here (pp. 247–258).

Angry Reactions

The most common resistance from the outside is anger.

- Why do some people react to others' boundaries with anger?

- How do you want to respond to people who are angry with you for setting healthy limits for yourself? Who, as a result of your boundaries, are not getting what they want? See Proverbs 19:19.

- Review the six steps for coping with someone's anger (pp. 248–249). Which step(s) calls for new behavior? Which step(s) offers you hope? What will you do to internalize these steps and make them your own? When will you take action?

Developing Healthy Boundaries

People who get angry at others for setting boundaries have a character problem. Self-centered, they think the world exists for them and their comfort. If you keep your boundaries, those who are angry at you will have to learn self-control for the first time, rather than using their anger to control other people (Jonah 4:9–11) (p. 249).

- People who get angry may leave their relationship with you if they can no longer control you. How does God run that risk with you and me everyday? Are you willing to take that risk with the angry, controlling people in your life? Why or why not?

God says he will only do things the right way and that he will not participate in evil. When people choose their own ways over his, he lets them go. Sometimes we have to do the same in our relationships (p. 249).

Guilt Messages

No weapon in the arsenal of the controlling person is as strong as the guilt message. People with poor boundaries almost always internalize guilt messages leveled at them. Controlling people who direct guilt messages at you are trying to make you change your choices. Remember the landowner's words in the parable of the workers in the vineyard: "Don't I have the right to do what I want with my own money?" (Matt. 20:15). The Bible says that we are to give and not be self-centered. It does not say that we have to give whatever anyone wants from us. We are in control of our giving. We are free to make our own choices, and we are to take responsibility for their impact on us and other people (pp. 249–252).

- What guilt messages (some are listed on pages 249–250) have been directed at you? By whom?

- What guilt messages are you dealing with today?

- Review the six steps for coping with guilt messages (pp. 251–252). Which step(s) gives you new insight into the dynamics of guilt messages? Be specific about what you've learned. Which step(s) calls for new behavior? Which step(s) offers you hope? What will you do to internalize these steps and make them your own? When will you take action?

Empathize with the distress the guilt sender is feeling, but make it clear that it is their distress. Stop reacting (Prov. 25:28). Give empathy. Be a listener, but don't take the blame. Make sure that the guilt sender hears that you hear the feeling behind the guilt message (p. 252).

Consequences and Countermoves

The consequences of setting boundaries will be countermoves by controlling people, and those can be harsh (p. 252).

- Who in your life will react like Brian's father by setting boundaries? Figure out what you are getting for your lack of boundaries and what you stand to lose by setting boundaries.

You face a risk in setting boundaries and gaining control of your life. The Bible is clear: Know the risk and prepare (Matt. 7:24–27; 2 Tim. 3:12). Follow Peter's example as you set boundaries and deal with the power moves of others: fix your eyes on Jesus (Matt. 14:29; Heb. 12:2). Look to him for help (Ps. 18:34), and know that he will be there to match your efforts (pp. 253–254).

- Review the remaining five steps for coping with the consequences of your boundary setting (pages 253–254). Which step(s) gives you helpful insights into the seriousness of the boundaries you are considering setting? Be specific about what you've learned. Which step(s) calls for new behavior? Which step(s) offers you strength? What will you do to internalize these steps and make them your own? When will you take action?

Physical Resistance

Some people can't maintain their boundaries with other people because they will be physically overpowered or injured. Physical abuse is a serious problem, and the abuser requires outside help. The problem will not go away, and it could get much worse. Seek help immediately (pp. 254–255).

- If you are in relationship with an abusive spouse or boyfriend, what is God's message to you in this section?

- When will you take action?

Pain of Others

When we begin to set boundaries with people we love, a really hard thing happens: they hurt. When you are dealing with someone who is hurting, remember that your boundaries are both necessary for you and helpful for them (Prov. 27:6) (p. 255).

- Whose pain is deterring you from setting and/or keeping boundaries?

- What message does this section have for you?

Blamers

Blamers will act as though your saying no is killing them, and they will react with a "How could you do this to me?" message. They are likely to cry, pout, or get angry. Listen to the nature of other people's complaints. If they are trying to blame you for something they should take responsibility for, confront them. If they have been hurt by something you've said or done, take action to restore the relationship (pp. 255–256).

- Are there blamers in your life? Whom do you expect to be a blamer once you set and maintain some boundaries?

- How will you respond?

Real Needs

You may need to set boundaries on people in real need. If you are a loving person, it will break your heart to say no to someone you love who is in need. But there are limits to what you can and cannot give. Empathize with people in need. Help them according to your own resources (Eph. 4:7). Send them to those who can help them. And pray for them. This is the most loving thing you can do for the pain and needs around you that you can't meet (p. 256).

- When has someone who loves you had to say no to you? How did you respond? With your better understanding of healthy limits and boundaries, how would you respond today?

- We encourage you to learn what your limits are. In what areas of your life are you flirting with burnout? Where do you need to—like Moses—follow Jethro's advice and delegate (Exod. 18)?

- How do you want to deal with the situation when you aren't able to give to someone you love?

Forgiveness and Reconciliation

Many people have a problem determining the difference between forgiveness and reconciliation (p. 256).

- Summarize the difference between forgiveness and reconciliation.

Forgiveness takes just one person; reconciliation takes two. We always need to forgive, but we don't always achieve reconciliation (Rom. 12:18; Matt. 10:35–36). God is your model. You can forgive someone and offer reconciliation, but reconciliation must be contingent upon that person owning his or her behavior and bringing forth fruits that indicate repentance and trustworthiness (pp. 257–258).

- Where have you or are you confusing forgiveness and reconciliation in your life? Whom do you need to forgive but not necessarily reconcile with?

Internal Resistances

We need good boundaries internally, as well as externally, if we are to say no to the flesh that wants to have dominion over us (Rom. 7:14; Matt. 26:41). Let's look at boundaries in regard to our internal resistance to growth (p. 258).

Human Need

God has designed us with very specific needs that are to be met in the family in which we grow up. Sadly, that doesn't always happen. But our unmet childhood needs can be met in the body of Christ (Ps. 68:6). When that happens, we will be strong enough to fight the boundary fights of adult life (pp. 258–259).

- What unmet childhood needs have resulted in broken places inside you? Be as specific as possible.

- How are these unmet needs interfering with your efforts to develop and maintain healthy boundaries?

- What are you doing—or what will you do—to have these needs met in a healthy way?

Unresolved Grief and Loss

If the "unmet needs" resistance has to do with getting the "good," grief has to do with letting go of the "bad" (Eccl. 7:2–4) (p. 259).

- The Bible is full of examples of God asking people to "leave behind" the people and lives that are not good for them. What do you need to leave behind?

The basic rule in biblical growth is that the life before God is not worth holding on to; we must lose it, grieve it, and let go so that he can give us good things (Phil. 3:8) (p. 259).

- What "if onlys" are you playing with instead of working on setting boundaries?

Giving up boundaries to get love postpones the inevitable: the realization of the truth about the person, the embracing of the sadness of that truth, and the letting go and moving on in life. You will be amazed by how much can change in your life when you finally begin to let go of what you can never have. Letting go is the way to maturity, and grief is the path (Eccl. 7:2) (pp. 260–261).

- Review the six steps you need to take to deal with unresolved grief and loss (pp. 260–261). Which step(s) gives you helpful insights? Be specific about what you've learned. Which step(s) calls for new behavior? Which step(s) offers you strength? What will you do to internalize these steps and make them your own? When will you take action?

Internal Fears of Anger

If angry people can make you lose your boundaries, you probably have an angry person in your head that you still fear (Matt. 10:28) (p. 262).

- How do you generally respond to an angry person? Do you have an angry person in your head? Who is that person?

A hurt, frightened part of you needs to be exposed to the light and the healing of God and his people. You need love to allow you to let go of the angry parent and stand up to the adults you now face. God does not want angry people to control you. He wants to be your master, and he doesn't want to share you with anyone (p. 262).

- Review the nine steps you need to take to face your fear of anger (pp. 262–263). Which step(s) calls for new behavior? What will you do to internalize these steps and make them your own? And when will you take action?

Fear of the Unknown

Another powerful internal resistance to setting boundaries is fear of the unknown. Being controlled by others is a safe prison. We know where all the rooms are. Boundaries open up all sorts of new options, and that can be scary. Yet, along with the fear, you find yourself stretched to new heights, possibilities, and realizations about God, yourself, and the world (pp. 263–264).

- The Bible has many stories about people called by God out of the familiar to an unknown land. He promises them that, if they step out in faith, he will lead them to a better land (Heb. 11:8). When have you had the opportunity to step out in faith? What did you do and what did you learn from that experience?

- Where is God calling you to step out now?

- In general, how do you deal with change?

- Review the nine steps you need to take to deal with your fear of the unknown (pp. 264–267). Which step(s) gives you helpful insights? Be specific about what you've learned. Which step(s) calls for new behavior? Which step(s) offers you strength? What will you do to internalize these steps and make them your own? When will you take action?

As you venture into the unknown, remember who God is and what he has shown us in his Son. He did not do that for nothing: he did it for our redemption and our future (Eph. 2:10) (p. 267).

Unforgiveness

"To err is human, to forgive is divine." And to not forgive is the most stupid thing we can do (p. 267).

- Why is forgiveness hard for you? What do you tend to do to collect on the debts that you have on the "books" of your soul?

Nothing is wrong with wanting debts resolved. The problem is that things will get resolved in only one way: with grace and forgiveness. To forgive is to render the account of the person who hurt you "canceled" (Col. 2:14) (p. 268).

- What grieving will you have to do if you forgive those who owe you for some past hurt?

- Again, explain the distinction between forgiveness and reconciliation.

If someone repents and then sins again, I will forgive, seventy times seven. But I want to be around people who honestly fail me, not dishonestly deny that they have hurt me and have no intent to do better. That is destructive for me and for them (p. 269).

- Whom do you need to forgive? Name the sin against you and then forgive it.

Gain grace from God and let others' debts go. Do not keep seeking a bad account. Let it go, then go and get what you need from God and people who can give (p. 269).

External Focus

People tend to look outside of themselves for the problem. This external perspective keeps you a victim. It says you can never be okay until someone else changes (2 Cor. 5:10). Look at yourself honestly and face the internal resistance of wanting the problem to be on the outside of you (pp. 269–270).

- What and/or whom are you blaming for your boundary problems rather than taking responsibility for them yourself?

- What are you doing that is keeping you boundaryless?

- What specific steps of confession and repentance will you take toward changing your boundarylessness? To whom will you confess? What change in behavior will you undertake?

Guilt

Guilt is a state of internal condemnation. It is the punitive nature of our fallen conscience saying, "You are bad," and it comes mainly from what we were taught in our early socialization process. We need to be careful about letting guilt feelings tell us we're wrong, for often the guilt feelings themselves are wrong (p. 270).

- Guilt feelings are not inerrant. They can appear when we have not done anything wrong at all, but have violated some internal standard that we have been taught. What internal standards were you taught growing up (i.e., "Don't say no," "Rescue people in need") that cause guilt when you violate them today—even though what you've done isn't wrong?

- To avoid unhealthy guilt, you must first realize that the guilt is your problem. Explain why people can't make you feel guilty.

- Review the ten steps you need to take to deal with this kind of false guilt (p. 266). Which step(s) gives you helpful insights? Be specific about what you've learned. Which step(s) calls for new behavior? Which step(s) offers you strength? What will you do to internalize these steps and make them your own? When will you take action?

Do not let guilt be your master any longer. We are to be motivated by love. When we are, what results when we fail is "godly sorrow" (2 Cor. 7:10), not unhealthy guilt rooted in our growing up years. Also, learn God's ways. Doing so can restore your soul and make your heart rejoice instead of feeling that controlling, parental guilt (pp. 271–272).

Abandonment Fears: Taking a Stand in a Vacuum

If one does not have secure bonding, setting boundaries is too frightening. Many people stay in destructive relationships because they fear abandonment (p. 272).

- Is the lack of secure bonding one reason why setting boundaries is frightening for you? Who are you afraid will abandon you if you set boundaries?

- A good support group is crucial to your efforts to establish and maintain healthy boundaries. What safe people are you — or can you — surrounding yourself with so that you can develop healthy bonds?

Being "rooted and grounded" (Eph. 3:17) in love in the body of Christ and with God will be the developmental fuel you need to risk boundary setting (p. 272).

If It Were Easy, You Would Have Done It By Now

Jesus warned, "In this world you will have trouble" (John 16:33), and that is what this lesson has been about. When you begin to do things Jesus' way, you will encounter trouble—from both outside and inside (p. 273).

- The world, the Devil, and even your own flesh will resist you and pressure you as you begin to hammer out a godly identity. What are the primary sources of pressure—both internal and external—you are encountering as you work on your boundaries?

As Jesus offered the warning above, he also offered hope: "But take heart! I have overcome the world" (John 16:33) (p. 273).

- To live life right, with healthy boundaries, is difficult (Matt. 7:14), but running into resistance is a good sign that you are doing what you need to do. In the following passages, what further hope do you find for fighting the battle to set and keep healthy limits?

  • James 1:2–4

  • 1 Peter 1:9

You are not alone in encountering external and internal resistances as you attempt to live a godly life. Your brothers and sisters in Christ, throughout the ages, have faced many trials as they ventured out on the road of faith, seeking a better land. As you travel on this journey—one that it is always riddled with trouble—know that your Good Shepherd promises to carry you through if you do your part (p. 273).

Prayer

Thank you, God, that what is right — boundaries, limits — is good for us. May I trust that statement even as I work toward experiencing that truth. It is good to know that you are with me as I fight both the external and the internal resistances to boundaries.

And, Lord, you know where the battles rage most intensely. You know the resistances from outside me — the angry reactions, the guilt-inducing statements, the counter-moves, the things I'm being blamed for, the risk of physical abuse, the pain that my no can mean to people I love, the real needs I'm unable to meet, and the struggle to forgive but not necessarily reconcile.

You also know my deep-rooted internal resistance to boundaries — my very real human needs that were never met during my childhood years, the guilt-inducing self-critic that took up residence in my head during those years, my unresolved grief and loss, and my fear of anger, of the unknown, of being abandoned if I set healthy limits. You also know where I am guilty of unforgiveness, and where I am failing to take responsibility and instead focusing outside me.

Now, may I come to truly know you — who knows all this and more about me — as my loving, protective Shepherd who will carry me through as I continue on this road toward biblical and healthy boundaries. I pray in Jesus' name. Amen.

Chapter 13

Success with Boundaries

Specific, orderly changes herald the emerging of mature boundaries. The eleven steps we'll look at in this lesson will help you to see where you are in your development and guide you to the next step. Then, like Jean, you will experience the rewards of setting and maintaining clear boundaries in your life. It requires hard work and risk-taking, but you'll find the effort worth it (p. 276).

Step #1: Resentment — Our Early-Warning Signal

Just as radar signals the approach of a foreign missile, your anger, resentment, or frustration can alert you to boundary violations in your life (Prov. 30:21–22) (p. 277).

- You have to be able to feel the anger when you're violated, manipulated, or controlled. Do you give yourself permission to feel angry? Are you aware of when you're being violated? Can you hear the early-warning signal?

If you answered no to these questions, find a safe place to learn to tell the truth. Keep in mind that our inability to feel anger is generally a sign that we are afraid of the separateness that comes with telling the truth. But when we acknowledge that truth is always our friend, we often give ourselves permission to be angry. When you are able to be honest about differences and disagreements, you will be better able to allow your anger to help you recognize where your boundaries are weak or nonexistent so that you can work on establishing firmer ones. You may even be able to, like Randy, recognize certain moments of anger as seeds for boundaries (pp. 276–277).

- What experiences or relationships helped you get in touch with your anger, resentment, or frustration and enabled you to see that you wanted to be treated differently?

Step #2: A Change of Tastes — Becoming Drawn to Boundary-Lovers

As boundary-injured individuals begin developing their own boundaries, they become attracted to people who can hear their no without being critical. Without getting hurt. Without personalizing it. Without running over their boundaries in a manipulative or controlling fashion (p. 279).

- In the past, how have you responded to people who can say a clear no? How do you respond now? How do you want to respond? At this time, are you able to see people who can say no—people you might once have labeled curt and cold—as caring and refreshingly honest?

We were created free for one basic purpose: to love, to be meaningfully close to God and to others (Col. 3:14). Because boundaries can't develop in a vacuum, we need to join with boundary lovers in deep, meaningful attachments. In fact, as you develop boundaries, you will find yourself attracted to boundary-lovers because, in them, you will find permission to be an honest, authentic, loving individual (p. 279).

- Explain how being able to say no fuels a loving and wholehearted yes.

- Who are the boundary-lovers in your life? If your list is short, where will you go to find some boundary-lovers?

Step #3: Joining the Family

Why is it so important to join the boundaried family? Because we need others with the same biblical values of limit setting and responsibility to encourage us, practice with us, and stay with us. With our awareness of people who believe in us and knowing that Jesus' Spirit is with us (Matt. 18:20), we can keep firm boundaries because we know we have a spiritual and emotional home somewhere (pp. 280–281).

- When has the friendship of someone with similar biblical values helped you stand strong? Be specific.

- How could being part of a boundaried family help you with your boundaries?

- Have you taken this step and joined the family of boundaried people? Describe the support group you have developed for yourself as you continue to work on your boundaries.

- If you have joined the family of boundaried people, how has their support helped you with your boundaries? Give two or three examples, perhaps referring to situations like Wayne's.

Step #4: Treasuring Our Treasures

After you feel safe with people who believe that grace and truth are good (John 1:17), you will begin to see that taking responsibility for yourself is healthy and that taking responsibility for other adults is destructive (p. 281).

- Scripture teaches that "we love because he first loved us" (1 John 4:19). In other words, we learn to be loving because we are loved. What did you learn about your worth, your lovableness, as a child?

God is interested in people loving others, and you can't love others unless you have received love inside yourself (p. 283).

- As a result of the childhood lessons you just referred to, how well do you take care of yourself—your feelings, talents, thoughts, attitudes, behavior, body, and resources God has entrusted to you? Support this answer with details from your life that show how well you take care of yourself or where you could improve.

Our basic sense of ourselves, of what is real and true about us, comes from our significant, primary relationships. Helen did not treasure herself because she had been sexually abused by her father—one of the people who should have cherished her most. She had no sense that she—or that any aspect of her—was a "pearl of great value" (Matt. 13:46) (pp. 281–282).

- Read 1 Corinthians 8:11. Why was Steve (pp. 282–283) excited about this verse? Have you, like Steve, been taught that protecting your spiritual and emotional property is selfish? What, then, does this verse say to you?

- Begin a list of your "treasures"—your time, money, feelings, and beliefs. How do you want others to treat them? How do you want others to *not* treat them?

God calls you to "above all else, guard your heart, for it is the wellspring of life" (Prov. 4:23). You are to value your treasures so much that you protect them (p. 283).

Step #5: Practicing Baby No's

Growth in setting emotional boundaries must always be at a rate that takes into account your past injuries. It is therefore wise to start small (p. 284).

- Shareen's mother sent guilt messages whenever Shareen set limits, and her father was enraged whenever she dared disagree. What past injuries make setting limits and saying no difficult for you?

When experiences in the past have taught you not to set limits, confronting someone on a relatively insignificant matter is never a small step—it's a huge leap forward (p. 284).

- But that huge leap must be taken only with careful planning. With who can you practice saying no? What support group and/or good friend(s) will you seek out to work on boundaries with? When will you take that step?

Begin practicing your no with people who will honor it and love you for it. Remember, too, that true intimacy is built on the freedom to disagree (Prov. 10:18) (p. 285).

Step #6: Rejoicing in the Guilty Feelings

As strange as it may seem, a sign that you're becoming a boundaried person is often a sense of self-condemnation, a sense that you've transgressed some important rules in your limit setting. If your conscience were silent and providing no "how could you?" guilt-inducing messages, it might mean that you were remaining enslaved to the internal parent. That's why we encourage you to rejoice in the guilt. It means you're moving ahead (p. 285).

- What evidence is there that you have a weak conscience or an overactive and unbiblically harsh internal judge (1 Cor. 8:7)? Give specific examples of the kind of condemning self-talk that goes on in your mind, or refer to people who have helped you recognize that you are not a very good friend to yourself.

- In what boundary setting will you feel like you are transgressing when you aren't? What are you going to do with that guilt?

Step #7: Practicing Grownup No's

Straightening out the extremely complicated, conflicted, frightening relationships in your life is a major goal in becoming a boundaried person and a step that requires some grownup no's (pp. 286–287).

- Who is your number one "boundary buster"? Who is the foremost person in your life with whom it's difficult to set limits? List all the names that come to mind.

Before considering what to do with these people, make sure that your goals for this important boundary work are not confused (p. 286).

- According to the discussion on page 286 and the Scriptures given there, what is the ultimate goal of boundary work?

The goal is to have a character structure that has boundaries and that can set limits on self and with others at the appropriate times. Furthermore, having internal boundaries results in having boundaries in the world (Prov. 23:7 NASB). Such Christlike maturity comes with lots of work, practice, and prayer (p. 287).

- Prayerfully make a list of your significant relationships. Now next to each name note the specific treasures that are being violated in these relationships. What specific boundaries do you need to set to protect these treasures?

- As always, be sure you aren't taking this step toward healthy boundaries alone. Who will support you as you take this critical step?

Developing a well-defined, honest, and goal-oriented character structure enables you to take this crucial step. That structure will also enable you to deal with any crisis that your boundaries may precipitate. Remember that the conflicts and disagreements that appear already exist. Boundaries simply bring them to the surface (p. 287).

Step #8: Rejoicing in the Absence of Guilty Feelings

Now that you are no longer listening to your internal parent, and are responding instead to the biblical values of love, responsibility, and forgiveness, you will notice the guilt generated by your formerly weak and overactive conscience diminishing (1 Tim. 3:9) (p. 287).

- Are you noticing an easing up of guilty feelings and an increase of empathic sorrow? Point to a specific instance of setting limits that might have caused you greater guilt and more self-recriminations had it happened before you started setting boundaries.

- Also identify some of the people that God has placed in your life and some of the situations he has seen you through which have helped quiet your harsh internal parent.

If you've been working through the steps outlined so far, you have had many experiences with people who understand love, responsibility, and forgiveness. As a result, your heart now has somewhere else to go for self-evaluation other than a critical conscience. Your heart can rest instead in the emotional memories of loving, truthful people. There is nothing to fuel guilt feelings (p. 287).

Step #9: Loving the Boundaries of Others

If we expect others to respect our boundaries, we need to respect theirs. Loving others' boundaries confronts our selfishness, increases our capacity to care about them, and teaches us empathy. We should fight for the no of others just as we should fight for our own no—even if it costs us something (pp. 288–289).

- How do you tend to respond to others' boundaries?

- We are commanded to love our neighbors as ourselves (Gal. 5:14). In light of this command, how would you like to respond to other people's boundaries?

Step #10: Freeing Our No and Our Yes

When people with undeveloped limit-setting abilities are unsure about something, they say yes. The fruit of maturing boundaries is being able to say no when you're unsure (p. 289.

- Think about the last time someone asked you for something you weren't sure you could give with a cheerful heart (2 Cor. 9:7). How did you respond? And how did you feel as you lived out your yes or your no?

Boundary-injured individuals who don't count the cost (Luke 14:28–30), or don't trust their conclusions if they do, make promises and then either resentfully make good or fail on them. You need to learn not to promise too much before you have done your spiritual and emotional calculations. When you are as free to say no to a request as you are to say yes, you are well on the way to boundary maturity (p. 289).

- What do you plan to do the next time someone asks you for something that you aren't sure you can give?

Step #11: Mature Boundaries — Value-Driven Goal Setting

The ultimate goal of learning boundaries is to free us up to protect, nurture, and develop the lives God has given us stewardship over. Setting boundaries is mature, proactive, and initiative-taking. It's being in control of our lives (pp. 291–292).

- What part of the glimpse into Ben and Jan's lives (pp. 290–291) is appealing to you? What aspects of their lives remind you of your own?

Individuals with mature boundaries aren't frantic, in a hurry, or out of control. They have a direction in their lives, a steady moving toward their personal goals. They plan ahead (p. 291).

- Now consider your life. Does your life tend toward a frantic or a steady pace? Does life feel in a hurry or out of control, or do you feel as if you're making steady progress toward a goal? How do your boundaries—or lack of them—contribute to the state of your life?

The reward for wise boundaries is the joy of desires fulfilled in life. It's being able to say, as Paul did, "The time has come for my departure. I have fought the good fight, I have finished the race, I have kept the faith" (2 Tim. 4:6–7) (pp. 291–292).

- Even as you mature, you will face all sorts of resistance to your boundaries and goals. What will you do to stand strong against this resistance? What weapons do you now have in your arsenal?

People with mature boundaries know that they will face resistance to their limits. They also know that, should it be needed, a no is waiting inside the heart—ready to be used not for an attack, not to punish, but to protect and develop the time, talents, and treasures that God has allocated to them (Ps. 90:10) (p. 292).

A Day in a Life with Boundaries

Remember Sherrie from chapter 1? She was stumbling through the day in a hap-hazard, out-of-control fashion. But then imagine that she has read this book, and has made significant progress. Look again at a day in her life now that she has boundaries (pp. 293–302).

- Where do you see in Sherrie's boundary-making actions things that you yourself are now doing?

- Where do you see in Sherrie's boundary-making actions and in the fruit of her boundary-making some goals for yourself? Be specific.

- Comment on Sherrie's prayer conversations with God. What in her comments to her heavenly Father is new and/or especially freeing for you?

- List some areas in which Sherrie has taken ownership in her life. To what do you attribute her success?

- Review the following aspects of Sherrie's life.
  - Her healthier sleep patterns
  - Her relationship with her mother
  - Her diet and exercise program
  - Her perspective that dieting and exercise is good stewardship, not selfishness
  - Her parenting: bedtimes for the children; shared household tasks; letting the children be responsible for getting to the carpool ride on time
  - Her work: her punctuality; her promotion; the boss she once covered for now being her assistant
  - Her friendship with Lois
  - Her family time: letting the answering machine protect mealtimes; mother-daughter walks
  - Her marriage: parenting together; setting limits with her husband and standing by clearly defined consequences; being more of a team with their new sense of mutual love and mutual responsibility; being unafraid of conflict; forgiving of each other's mistakes; being respectful of each other's boundaries
  - Her limits on and wiser choices with church commitments
  - Her relationship with God
  - Her strong support group

- In which of the areas listed have you seen progress in your own life? Take time, as Sherrie did, to thank God!

- In which of the areas listed do you still have work to do? What boundary work are you doing in those areas? Be specific about your plan and your current efforts in regard to these issues.

Sherrie's example is not a fairy-tale fantasy. It's a real-life experience that you yourself can experience and perhaps already are experiencing. Like Sherrie, you can learn to take ownership of your life. You can learn what things are your responsibility and what are not. You can stop taking on problems that God never intended you to take on. You can learn to live by biblical boundaries and experience the relationships and achieve the purposes that God intends for you. As you know, it has been our prayer for you that your biblical boundaries will lead you to a life of love, freedom, responsibility, and service (pp. 293–302).

Prayer

God, you know where I am on this journey toward healthy boundaries. You know which of the eleven steps I've taken and which lie ahead.

I thank you for the anger you built into me to warn me of boundary violations. Teach me to pay attention to those internal signals. Open my eyes to the boundary-lovers around me and help me to learn from them. Thank you for the blessing of a support group and the valuable lessons and love the people in it offer me. And thank you for your love and for the worth I can find in you, despite childhood lessons I learned about my lack of worth.

Give me courage to practice my baby no's — and give me wisdom as I choose people to practice with. Thank you that I can rejoice in my guilt, knowing that your rules for living are better than the rules that I learned growing up, the rules that generate these messages of guilt. Give me courage to confront the boundary-busters in my life with grownup no's.

Thank you for the knowledge that someday the guilt will be gone and for that sign of health, that sign of your loving and healing faithfulness in my life. Teach me to love others as myself and to respect their boundaries the way I want them to respect mine. And teach me to count the cost when I see an opportunity to give, and then to freely say yes or just as freely say no.

Finally, it is my prayer that you will continue to help me learn to take ownership of my life, to teach me to see what is my responsibility and what isn't, to show me what problems I've taken on that you never intended for me, and to guide me as I try to establish and live by biblical boundaries. May I live a life of love, freedom, responsibility, and service to your glory. I pray in Jesus' name. Amen.

EMBARK ON A
LIFE-CHANGING JOURNEY
OF PERSONAL AND SPIRITUAL GROWTH

DR. HENRY CLOUD   **DR. JOHN TOWNSEND**

Dr. Henry Cloud and Dr. John Townsend have been bringing hope and healing to millions for over two decades. They have helped people everywhere discover solutions to life's most difficult personal and relational challenges. Their material provides solid, practical answers and offers guidance in the areas of *parenting, singles issues, personal growth,* and *leadership.*

Bring either Dr. Cloud or Dr. Townsend to your church or organization. They are available for:

- Seminars on a wide variety of topics
- Training for small group leaders
- Conferences
- Educational events
- Consulting with your organization

Other opportunities to experience Dr. Cloud and Dr. Townsend:

- Ultimate Leadership workshops—held in Southern California throughout the year
- Small group curriculum
- Seminars via Satellite
- Solutions Audio Club—Solutions is a weekly recorded presentation

For other resources, and for dates of seminars and workshops
by Dr. Cloud and Dr. Townsend, visit:
www.cloudtownsend.com

For other information **Call (800) 676-HOPE (4673)**

Or write to:
Cloud-Townsend Resources
18092 Sky Park South, Suite A
Irvine, CA 92614

Boundaries in Marriage

Understanding the Choices That Make or Break Loving Relationships

*Dr. Henry Cloud
and Dr. John Townsend*

Only when you and your mate know and respect each other's needs, choices, and freedom can you give yourselves freely and lovingly to one another. *Boundaries in Marriage* gives you the tools you need. Drs. Henry Cloud and John Townsend, counselors and authors of the award-winning bestseller *Boundaries*, show you how to apply the principles of boundaries to your marriage. This long-awaited book helps you understand the friction points or serious hurts and betrayals in your marriage — and move beyond them to the mutual care, respect, affirmation, and intimacy you both long for.

Hardcover, Jacketed: 978-0-310-22151-7
Softcover: 978-0-310-24314-4

Workbook: 978-0-310-22875-2
DVD: 978-0-310-27813-9
Participant's Guide: 978-0-310-24615-2

Pick up a copy today at your favorite bookstore!

Boundaries in Dating

How Healthy Choices Grow Healthy Relationships

*Dr. Henry Cloud
and Dr. John Townsend*

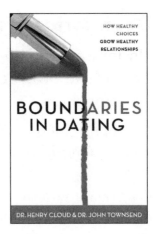

Boundaries in Dating provides a way to think, solve problems, and enjoy the benefits of dating in the fullest way, including increasing the ability to find and commit to a marriage partner.

Softcover: 978-0-310-20034-5

Pick up a copy today at your favorite bookstore!